Selling Your Business for More

Selling Your Business for More

Maximizing Returns for You, Your Family, and the Business

Daniel R. Barron
Mary Geddes Boehler
and
Marian F. Cook

First published in 2010 by
PALGRAVE MACMILLAN®
in the United States—a division of St. Martin's Press LLC,
175 Fifth Avenue, New York, NY 10010.

Where this book is distributed in the UK, Europe and the rest of the world, this is by Palgrave Macmillan, a division of Macmillan Publishers Limited, registered in England, company number 785998, of Houndmills, Basingstoke, Hampshire RG21 6XS.

Palgrave Macmillan is the global academic imprint of the above companies and has companies and representatives throughout the world.

Palgrave® and Macmillan® are registered trademarks in the United States, the United Kingdom, Europe and other countries.

ISBN: 978–0–230–61893–0

Library of Congress Cataloging-in-Publication Data is available from the Library of Congress.

A catalogue record of the book is available from the British Library.

Design by Newgen Imaging Systems (P) Ltd., Chennai, India.

First edition: February 2010

10 9 8 7 6 5 4 3 2 1

Printed in the United States of America.

To our families for making this journey with us,
especially Bill, Shawn, and Zoe

Contents

Figures

Foreword

David Lansky

As an advisor to business owners and their families, my work is centered around supporting my clients in their efforts to keep those businesses thriving through multiple generations or helping my clients successfully navigate the life-changing transition involved in selling a business outside the family and moving on. For many baby boom generation entrepreneurs, selling their business at the right time and in the right way is the preferred decision.

Realizing financial value from years, or even generations, of dedication to a family business can be an overwhelmingly positive event in the lives of business owners and their families. But a transition of this magnitude is much more than a business transaction. To be done well requires thoughtful, thorough planning and preparation for the owner, the business, and all the stakeholders, and it requires disciplined execution and a tailored design for transition after the sale.

Successful entrepreneurs and business owners occasionally believe that their talent in founding and/or successfully running a business will easily translate to the tasks of an outside sale. This is not the case much of the time, and I have often thought that an objective guide would be a most helpful resource in identifying tasks, skill gaps, and areas where outside advice is essential.

This book walks you through a values-based approach to designing and carrying out a comprehensive and integrated exit plan. Planning chapters cover specific steps to help you clarify your objectives and desired outcomes for your employees, management, the legacy of your business, and, of course, your personal financial goals. You will find specific steps to take within your timeline to increase the value of your business before bringing it to market. There is a chapter devoted to financial planning and wealth transfer planning for you and your family before the sale begins, and it offers ideas and strategies that further your estate planning goals and charitable intent while mitigating taxes when the time comes to sell.

There is a piece on who the critical advisors are to help you market and sell your business smoothly and how to choose the right players for your needs and your team. Other chapters covering the marketing process and transaction itself demystify how an investment banker will operate. This book explains in a simple but thorough manner what to expect in the sale process, ranging from qualifying buyers, exercising due diligence in selecting a buyer, and to understanding the many documents involved in closing the deal. A transition chapter outlines the many new choices you will have to make once the deal is done, and how to address them, including managing your new wealth, moving on to a family enterprise, and whether to create a family office.

As this book is being written, we are barely beginning to emerge from the "Great Recession of 2009," a period when the distressed economy made selling a private business a very difficult exercise. If you are considering a sale as the Merger and Acquisition market grows more favorable, read this book and begin your preparation now.

Alignment and consensus among family members are key elements in the successful transition of family businesses. If you are planning a sale, it will be useful to pass this book along to family shareholders and family employees of your business. This can help assure that the right parties have a shared understanding of the path that will be followed as the process unfolds.

You owe it to yourself and your family to follow the principles laid out in this book to prepare you and your business for your future exit. By bringing your company to market at the best time with the optimal process, you will reap not only a superb financial reward but also realize the personal satisfaction of doing your best for all stakeholders involved.

Acknowledgments

Just as a business owner does not work alone, neither do authors. Many people have contributed to this book in ways large and small, graciously giving of their time and expertise.

Thank you to David Allen, Joe Carlin, Regina Carlin, Linda Darragh, Lisa Donovan, Robert Hamilton, Bob Jordan, Kris Kalter, Stephanie Kuhlen, David Lansky, Gerald LeVan, Kalli Mulvey, Mike Nikolich, Ann Ostrowski, Mary Taylor, Jim Teufel, David Tolmie, and Jeremy Weir.

We also thank our Northern Trust colleagues and the myriad business owners and advisors we have worked with and learned from over the years.

A special tip of the hat to our agents, Cynthia Zigmund and John Willig, for making the partnership with Palgrave Macmillan happen, and to Don Nichols for his sharp editing eye and help steering this project to completion. A special thanks to Jerry Mazurczak and, of course, our deep gratitude to our editor, Laurie Harting.

About the Authors

Daniel R. Barron is Managing Director of Northern Trust's Family Business Group. A certified American Society of Appraisers valuation expert, Dan brings more than twenty-one years of experience working with private businesses and the families that surround them. Dan has led numerous business sales and restructuring initiatives and has deep experience in developing planning strategies with his Northern Trust clients.

Mary Geddes Boehler brings the fiduciary and business transaction background as well as extensive experience in fully integrated business succession planning and estate planning for affluent clients. She has advised family business owners and their companies for fifteen years as Managing Director of Northern Trust Company's Family Business Group. Mary is currently an independent consultant to private business owners.

For twenty-five years, **Marian F. Cook** has been a trusted advisor to the hundreds of owners and executives worldwide whom she has helped to improve business performance and value. She has worked globally with firms ranging in size from start-ups to Fortune 500 companies. She has helped them develop and execute their strategies, realize their goals, and maximize their businesses' valuations and their transitions to new ownership. She has the perspective of a business owner herself as President and CEO of the management and technology consulting firm Ageos. Ageos specializes in business transitions, such as preparing the owner and business for sale and working with owners to achieve success as they define it.

Notes on Contributors

David Lansky is a senior consultant with The Family Business Consulting Group, Inc. and is a nationally recognized expert on the psychology and family dynamics of wealth and business. His regular column, "Money and Meaning," in the *Journal of Practical Estate Planning*, is read widely by trust and estate attorneys, financial planners, and other advisors.

Mike Nikolich is president of Tech Image, Chicago's leading independent technology public relations firm. He sold his business to Smith Bucklin in 2007 and will become chief marketing officer of the association management firm in 2010.

Introduction

The starting point or "ah-ha moment" for this book was the realization that, after decades in the business, we have yet to find a book that discussed how business owners' values influence the sale of their businesses. *Selling Your Business for More* takes a holistic approach to this subject. It recognizes what surveys and our experience have shown: selling a business is not a single event, nor is it solely about maximizing the price you receive. It is a process. The process begins with a decision to sell that may arise from a vague notion or a hard imperative or a judgment made when the business was founded. If entered into intelligently and guided properly, that process unfolds systematically and professionally with respect and fairness toward everyone involved. It ends the way it is designed to end—and that design is the result not only of clear thinking, good advice, and sound execution, but also of knowing *what* to think about, *whom* to consult, and *how* to execute. It is a process of slips, setbacks, and surprises, but if you are, or are about to be engaged, in that process, you have an advantage: others—especially your authors—have been there before. This book addresses the entire process of selling to assure that you and your family earn every reward from a change in ownership. And success is wrapped around what you, the seller, hold important. The dollar value you extract from your sale is a significantly important element, but the measure of your success is much more than just that number.

Written for owners of private small to midsized companies, *Selling Your Business for More* speaks to the realization these men and women face when they decide to sell their companies: business is more than a sequence of financial transactions, and so is selling it. Business is people and relationships inside and outside the organization. To be in business is to create something from nothing and to create something greater than yourself. The link between these larger issues and a business's everyday transactions is your values. This link is most apparent during "the ultimate transaction"—the process of selling your business. *Selling Your Business for More* deals with this "ultimate transaction" in the context of larger issues that perhaps you don't talk about but nonetheless feel in your bones.

If you are like most owners we have encountered, you will have three goals when selling your business:

- Getting the optimum financial value for your business within the framework of your values and tolerance for risk.
- Doing the right thing for your family, dedicated management, long-term employees, and the continuity of your business.
- Enjoying your success by planning a fulfilling post-sale life.

To address the more encompassing approach that you as a selling-owner need, *Selling Your Business for More* is organized into three sections. They are, first, preparing owners and the business for sale, second, conducting the sale, and third, designing and implementing the post-sale transition and wealth management strategies. Our contents include the following:

- Identifying your goals and alternatives
- Selecting the best buyer, deal structure, and selling strategy to meet those goals
- Decision criteria and analyzing the timing and type of deal best for your sale
- Optimizing and preparing your business to draw the highest selling price, followed by making a transition right for your business and your future
- Marketing and selling your business, including selection and management of the appropriate team
- Successfully transitioning your business to its new owners
- Post-sale planning with an emphasis on managing the sometimes-substantial liquid wealth from selling a business

We also have included a section on managing a successful integration if your business is merged with another organization. This process is distinctly different from simply changing owners, and it deserves a more thorough discussion.

This book is a collaboration by three of us who are seasoned and acknowledged authorities in the field. Each of us brings singular and complementary sets of expertise to this task. As experts, we understand the market and center our efforts upon achieving the best outcomes from a business, financial, and values-based orientation. In *Selling Your Business for More*, we offer proven, implementable solutions, starting with the moment you consider selling and continuing through assuring that you and your business thrive after sale. It is a comprehensive yet comprehensible guidebook for the transition from running your business into enjoying the next phase of your life.

Not a book of theory, it offers hard-learned examples from our experience to bring those lessons to life. We know that each business has its own nuances. That reality, coupled with the reality that markets and regulations change constantly, illustrates the need for a team of experts dedicated to the needs of each owner. This book cannot replace their situation-specific dedication and knowledge. We believe there are wisdom and a practical roadmap in these pages. But you still should engage the best advisors to advance your personal and professional situation.

Chapter 1, "Deciding to Sell," examines potential motivations for selling a business and addresses questions about the firm's salability, timing, and sales involving multiple owners.

Chapter 2, "Goals and Objectives for the Sale," leads sellers through the steps of understanding what they want to achieve personally and professionally from the sale of their business. It covers such subjects as defining "success," forming a preliminary picture of the owner's life after sale, and integrating the seller's vision of the business's continuing health into his or her own.

Chapter 3, "Managing People and Processes During Change," provides a synopsis of the key personnel and processes involved in selling a business and how they should be managed for an effective conclusion. It discusses the essential steps in selling, such as project management, leadership transition, documentation, and communication.

Chapter 4, "Preparing Your Company for Sale," is a comprehensive discussion of preparing a firm to be sold. The chapter focuses on its main point: before you sell, invest money and time in what makes your business more attractive and valuable. It offers concrete advice on the essential steps, including recasting financials, preparing documents, revisiting decision-making authority, diversifying the sales and customer base, and many other issues.

Chapter 5, "What Is It Worth? Valuing Your Business," guides sellers through the critical process of assessing their firm's worth in the market. It covers the common measures of valuation and provides detailed insight into the methods that appraisers and potential buyers use in reaching a valuation and sales price. It explains significant concepts such as why a strategic buyer will pay more and how minority and illiquid interests are valued, and it gives examples that assist sellers in frequently seen situations.

Selling a business generates a substantial sum of liquidity. Chapter 6, "Setting the Stage and Getting It Together Now to Enjoy Later," provides important suggestions for minimizing the taxman's take while securing the seller's estate and financial goals. It explains the use of trusts and philanthropic gifts and emphasizes the importance of arrangements to be made before a sale is consummated.

Selling a business is a team effort. Chapter 7, "Assembling Your Own A-Team," specifies who needs to be on the selling team, explains the roles each key member fills, and discusses the use of external advisors, including investment bankers and transaction attorneys.

Sometimes the interests of families, partners, and stakeholders and state of financial markets simply aren't conducive to a swift sale at attractive terms. Chapter 8, "Considering Alternatives: Special Situations," discusses impediments to a smooth sale and provides specific guidance for overcoming resistance and positioning a firm for a good sale at a bad time. It also discusses alternatives to an outright sale to a conventional buyer, such as sale of assets, recapitalizations, and management buyouts.

Chapter 9, "Timing Is Everything: Pulling the Trigger," asks and answers the question "When is the right time to bring a company to the market?" It deals in depth with "timing" as an issue of personal readiness and market receptiveness and provides a matrix for helping sellers make important timing decisions.

Chapter 10, "How to Engage the Market: Selecting the Best Process for Selling," explains the three general methods for selling a company and instructs sellers in choosing methods appropriate for their situation. It also discusses elements common to all three sales approaches, such as contacting buyers, evaluating offers, and negotiating the sale.

Chapter 11, "Preparing the Paperwork: Documents Attendant to Your Sale," is an extensive discussion of the documents sellers need for opening a sale, progressing through each step of negotiation, and concluding the agreement. Topics include the critical documents needed for a sale, including nondisclosure agreements, letters of intent, purchase/sale agreements, due diligence, and many others.

Merging a business with another, often larger, firm requires a completely different mentality and process from selling it to another individual. A true success for everyone in a merger situation means a successful integration of two firms after the sale. Chapter 12, "Greater Than the Sum of the Parts: Managing an Integration," is an extended, detailed discussion of the procedures, personnel, structures, and responsibilities that must be in place for a merger and integration to work.

Selling a business delivers a sometimes-huge sum of liquid wealth to sellers, their partners, and families. Chapter 13, "After the Close: Now What?," discusses the personal and professional transitions involved in selling a business and how to select advisors to assist. It discusses how sellers might wish to deploy their wealth, whether by finding a new business or creating a charitable foundation. In particular, the chapter provides an extensive discussion on choosing a wealth manager.

In the case study, "Successfully Selling Your Business Requires More Than Luck," discussed in the Afterword, a business owner's recent experience reinforces the main lessons of our book. The sale of his public relations firm did not succeed on the first try, yet that setback prepared him for the next time, which produced a very successful sale. A story told in his own words, the sale of his firm brings to life every lesson we've learned through our decades of serving business owners: timing the market is difficult, be prepared, look at your finances before you start the selling process, bring in top-drawer advisors, design a post-sale role in the business, expect setbacks and learn from them, position the company for sale, know the importance of communication, and understand your values and be guided by them.

CHAPTER 1

Deciding to Sell

Introduction

So you're thinking of selling your business? Why? Is it because the market is right or someone made an unexpected offer for your business, or you feel the need for a change? And who among us doesn't occasionally think about walking away from our jobs? But for business owners, a decision to sell is more complex. Your business represents your efforts, values, and vision in a way that no job could. As business writer Leigh Buchanan puts it, entrepreneurship is business at its most human and passionate level. At times all-consuming professionally and personally, your business is the result of many years of work and risk, and of dreams realized and dreams deferred.

Your business provides you with more than an income, whether you realize it or not. It also provides many ingredients for a fulfilling life: purpose, structure, validation, pride, friendships, and an impact on your community and family that may ripple through the generations. Life without your business—getting the big payout and relaxing on the beach—may seem like a shimmering paradise in the mind's eye, yet foreign and unattainable. How to get there from here? And what is the "there" there? You know what you're leaving, but where are you going? Transitioning from your familiar way of life into another takes planning, self-knowledge, and courage.

Some business owners sell the business and stride boldly into, well, nothing. They assume something will turn up. But entrepreneurs generally don't do "nothing" well, and they discover that golf really is not a long-term substitute for "something." Without a set purpose and goal, they flounder to find a meaningful, challenging, and enjoyable way to contribute. As the actress Helen Hayes once said, "If you rest, you rust."

Other business owners either haven't taken the time—or don't know how—to define what they'd like to do after selling their business, and that stops them from moving forward. Confusion and uncertainty about your post-sale life and the post-sale future of your business can produce paralyzing anxiety that delays important exit planning. The selling process and life after sale seem incomprehensible and downright scary. For many owners like you, this is a once-in-a-lifetime financial and emotional deal—one you may have little or no experience with and one with considerable long-term consequences. It's not surprising that most owners don't plan their exit as thoroughly as they could. They don't have a destination or a map to get there.

We spoke recently with a business owner who felt turned off by how narrow-minded previous advisors and their advice were. We weren't surprised at his comment. Most consultants and books look only at the transaction, not the holistic process, the person behind the sale, or what is important in the deal. If you, too, lack the fuller perspective from having a personal plan and comprehensive counsel, you may be forced to react to crises or events beyond your control instead of selling at your preferred time and terms. As the sale process begins and advances to an end, you may feel lost: the opportunity wasn't quite what you thought, and the result wasn't what you expected.

Questions about selling a business can overwhelm you. What do I want for myself and my family? What are my values, and how do I build them into the sales process? Can I sell? Why should I sell? What are my goals for the sale? What will I do after the sale? How does the market value my business compared to what I believe it's worth? Am I being realistic? Is the timing right? If I wait or make changes, will I get more? Do I want to invest the time and resources to get a higher price? Where will I find buyers who share my vision for the business? What can I do to assure a smooth transition and my business's long-term success after I've left? What about my employees? When and how do I tell them of the sale? How do I involve them in the process? How can I reward those people that have helped make this business a success? How will my clients and suppliers react to the news? These are only a few of many questions that will surface during the selling process. Let's begin by reviewing why you might consider making this momentous decision at all.

Reasons for Selling

You should have a compelling reason to sell. For one thing, without compelling motivation the deal likely won't happen. Many buyers will sense the lack of urgency or commitment and put on the brakes. Your business could get a reputation for being shopped around, and wasting others' time, and this perception in the marketplace could work against you when you are serious about selling. Additionally, selling a business is hard work not to be undertaken halfheartedly. You already have a full-time job and shouldn't take on more work without a compelling reason to do so.

And it does have risks. For example, you may need to make investments in the business and will need to reach out in confidence to key employees to assemble information buyers will want to see. If news of a potential sale leaks, it could create turbulence among employees and, if it's an external leak, among competitors, clients, and vendors. You should have a strong reason for taking on this work and risk. Although we have seen successful sales after a failed first round, it is difficult to relaunch the process and get the right buyers engaged.

And finally, prospective buyers understandably will be interested in why your business is on the market. It may very well be the first question they ask. Therefore, you should be able to explain your reasons crisply, consistently, and convincingly. Buyers will want a willing partner in this process who is as committed to its success as they are.

There are many reasons for selling a business. Generally, they fall into two categories: personal and professional.

Personal Reasons to Sell

Health and Age
The most common personal reasons for selling a business are health and age. With millions of baby boomer business owners looking to retire soon, this has never been more true; in fact, a significant portion of privately held firms are expected to change hands during the next ten years. After investing years of energy and ideas in their enterprise, their arc of business ownership is descending.

Many business owners have told us that the challenges and rewards of the business have added years to their lives. It is not uncommon to have business owners in their seventies still at the helm. For these fulfilled people, life, longevity, and business ownership are one and the same. On the other hand, we have seen cases where the stress of the business has nearly destroyed a business owner's health. We know of a company that did take its toll on the health of the owner. Once she sold her business, she needed to repair herself and recommit to her health. Her next venture was owning— not running—an organic restaurant.

Need for a Change
Another personal reason—need for a change—can prompt a sale and open a new direction and lifestyle for an owner. Business ownership is not for the faint of heart. Pressures of entrepreneurship are many and significant and can breed a craving to relieve burnout. The flip side of this is that owners who haven't made significant changes to their business or work routine can find themselves bored. Their business is not receiving the attention it had in the past, and selling it to someone with a fresh perspective and renewed energy could revitalize the seller and the business.

Some entrepreneurs thrive on the start-up phase of a business, and once it stabilizes they seek new challenges, frequently by selling. Not interested in sitting atop a well-oiled machine, they find their joy in creating something from nothing, and then selling it to professional managers who can take it to the next level. In other cases, the owner sees a lucrative opportunity elsewhere and needs to exit current responsibilities to pursue it.

Need for Liquidity

A third reason to sell can be your need or desire for personal liquidity. After years of building the business, it may be time to reap your rewards. The majority of business owners' net worth often is in their business. New circumstances or aspirations may mean extracting some or all of that net worth from the business. Often, owners started or bought a business intending to sell it profitably to fund other opportunities or retirement, and selling always offers an opportunity to redirect wealth toward new opportunities or interests. We know of many owners who never intended to run their business indefinitely, but to build and sell it, and then move to the next venture.

Despite a need or desire for liquidity, most business owners don't know the value of their business and, therefore, their own net worth and the opportunities for new ventures that selling provides. One of our recommendations later in the book will be to get that first benchmark valuation. Understanding how much money you realistically can expect from selling helps you to set expectations for the future you design for yourself.

Professional Reasons to Sell

Lack of Capital

One of the most common business-focused reasons to sell is lack of capital. Just as selling the business offers an increase in personal liquidity, it also can generate capital needed to expand the business or make changes needed for growth. It is not uncommon for a business owner to become more risk-averse over time and not borrow money to make potentially rewarding investments. The business can plateau as a result, or be leapfrogged by competitors who are willing to invest.

Financial Anxiety

A related reason to sell is that business ownership can be fraught with financial anxiety. Understandably, matters such as personal guarantees for the company's debts, product liability, and tax obligations can be overwhelming and prompt owners to sell. For some people, the rewards of being a business owner aren't worth its stresses.

Disputes with Co-Owners

Owner disputes can provoke the sale of a business, and they have profound effects on determining the timing, structure of the deal, and potential buyers. When businesses have multiple owners, there's always possibility for conflict. Owners may have differing visions of the business's direction, disagree on any number of issues, have differing needs for personal liquidity, or find their relationship has become unhealthy for the business.

Change in Market Conditions

A change in market or business conditions may trigger your decision to sell. Fearing that the market is nearing the top of the cycle may convince you to jump while the opportunity is hot. We were involved in several situations during the dot-com boom where business owners, stunned at what their businesses' were valued at, made their deals and their money and got out. Declining markets, regulatory changes, industry consolidation, or demand shifts are examples of situations that may make selling your business a smart move. New competitors, declining sales and profits, changing traffic patterns, or losing key employees, patents, suppliers, contracts, or clients don't necessarily mean the business itself will end, but perhaps a new owner is needed to make competitive adjustments. And, of course, sale of a business may be mandated by bankruptcy.

A Final Reason

The final reason for selling can be professional *and* personal, and quite common: lack of a qualified successor. A significant majority of business owners expect to keep the business in the family. At some point, many who anticipated passing their businesses to the next generation realize that, for whatever reasons, it won't happen. So they turn outside and seek a buyer.

Is Your Business Saleable?

If you are seriously considering selling, determining whether your business *can* be sold is clearly your first question. In the best-case scenario, buyers are looking for consistent and healthy profits and growth from a loyal and diverse customer base, preferably with long-term and profitable contracts. Attractive inventory and location for the future, limited competition, no legal entanglements, and physical assets—including offices and facilities—that are in good shape are all attractive to potential buyers. Strategic fit, a strong brand, intellectual property, and difficult-to-replicate products, processes, or people in a specialized work-force also make a business salable. Realistically, though, not all businesses have these assets and can be sold. Besides the inverse of the items above, there are other limiting factors such as an undocumented systems and processes, underinvesting in the business, and bad timing.

Undocumented Systems and Processes

For example, an owner may have built a business entirely around his personality, work habits, preferences, or lifestyle, which a new owner can't adapt. Perhaps systems, processes, and asset values are documented only in the current owner's mind, making it difficult to transfer operations and separate the business from the current owner. We know investment bankers who routinely ask a selling business owner if he knows how the database works or if he can fix the network. If the answer is "Yes," the bankers believe the business owner is too involved, the business cannot transfer easily and is therefore less attractive to them.

We worked with a professional services organization where the core service offering's process was never standardized or documented. Although the owners took pride in their "craftsman-like and customized approach" to each client, without standardization, documentation, or reusable tools, their quality was uneven and therefore less valuable, and hence not easily transferrable. Small professional services organizations also have an issue when the majority of their client rainmaking and relationships depend on the owner. Client relationships will have to be transferred carefully to retain client loyalty and business.

Underinvestment and Poor Timing

Perhaps erratic investment has caused disparate and disconnected assets to be bundled together haphazardly as "a business." A new owner could find it difficult to establish the business's value, much less optimize it in a going concern after the current owner departs.

Also, a seller may have waited too long. Perhaps the business or market has peaked and earlier performance doesn't reflect its future. Former or prospective changes in markets, regulations, and laws may diminish the value of a business, making it no longer worthwhile to purchase. In one heartbreaking situation we know of, the owner clung too long to the business. He enjoyed the prestige in the community his business brought him, and he could not envision a future without it. Over the years, the value of his business sank, and he lost a huge opportunity that had a generational impact on his family's wealth. In this case, the only option may be liquidation.

What Is It We're Selling?

As you think about selling your business, you need to get a clear understanding of what exactly it is that you are selling. Assuming that you are selling all of the business, instead of just a business unit or pieces of equipment, there are two general ways to do so: selling the entire business entity or selling the assets. Since, as we'll discuss later, this has implications from taxes to liabilities, it is important to understand them at a high level up front.

Selling the Business Entity, or Share Purchase

In this case, the buyer is purchasing the legal structure or business entity and all assets and liabilities by buying your firm's stock. The business is sold in its entirety as is, with everything that the business owns and owes—lock, stock, and barrel—without having to transfer individual assets and liabilities.

Asset Sale

In this second case, the buyer transfers the negotiated assets and only the liabilities associated with them into a new business entity. Buyers tend to prefer this kind of sale since it limits the liabilities they are purchasing.

Considerations for Multiple Owners

The laws governing business entities, including corporations, partnerships, joint ventures and limited liability companies, are complex and vary significantly from state to state. The governing jurisdiction, as well as the entity's charter documents and contractual relationships, will determine what duties and obligations the owners may have to each other (and other parties such as debt holders) in the context of the sale of a business. As part of the pre-sale planning process, the owners of the business should consult with legal counsel to address these considerations. It is crucial to determine what effect selling the business will have on the company's various owners and other stakeholders.

Understanding the legal constraints identified, each owner needs to do his or her own soul-searching regarding what it is he or she is looking for in the sale. This enables early and honest conversations between and among owners regarding the sale and expectations. Disagreeable, discordant, or adversarial owner relationships during the sale process could be disastrous. Agreeing on what is and isn't negotiable will assure that owners are working as a team toward the same goal.

If it is a dispute between owners that is driving the sale, it could become contentious. Owners working as a team toward the same goals are key to a successful sale. If the dispute causing the sale could complicate or negatively impact the sale and sales process, consider bringing in a mediator to help.

Multiple owners—either partners or other shareholders—are legally required to deal fairly with each other in all transactions, including sale of the business. For co-ownership within a partnership structure, state laws require partners to act with good faith toward each other and the partnership. All material facts must be disclosed. Just as during the normal course of business a partner is required to share benefits of the partnership, the same is true for sale of the business. In a general partnership, partners cannot benefit themselves to the detriment of other partners, although in limited partnerships the general partner may have more economic rights than limited partners. Each of these considerations depends on the operating agreement, which must be considered when you sell your business.

Most small or family-owned businesses are established as close corporations, which some states call "incorporated partnerships." Distinctions among partners or shareholders in this form of ownership are not great, and it's crucial to consider what effect selling the business will have on everyone concerned. Previously established buy-sell agreements often spell out what happens if a shareholder wishes to or must sell, becomes incapacitated, or dies. Agreements specify the valuation formula or process to be used to buy back shares or guarantee right-of-first-refusal for other shareholders. Frequently, voting trusts or other agreements declare who must approve important corporate decisions, including sale of assets. All established agreements must be respected or amended and reviewed by an attorney before offering your company for sale.

Is the Timing Right?

Selling your business at the right time can be a difficult call with a significant influence on its price. The best time to sell is when you don't have to: the business and industry are growing, and no uncontrolled event, personal need, or time constraint forces the sale. This frequently is beyond your control, however, and timing a market up-cycle can be difficult. Your attempt to time the cycle may cause you to wait, thinking things will be better next year, and miss the opportunity if the economy turns before expected.

Reasons for selling, such as health issues, divorce, and owner disputes, may drive the timing of the sale by accelerating it beyond what may be best for the business or you. The need or willingness to make a significant investment in the business to raise the price or make it attractive to the targeted buyer will push out the timing of the sale. The best case is the perfect timing of personal needs, business attractiveness, and market strength, and that rarely happens.

What you should resist is jumping at an unexpected offer. If a buyer appears with an offer too good to be true, it probably is. And even if it is on target, without a competitive process involving more than one offer, you will never know if you could have done better on the price, terms, or other elements of the deal. Reacting impulsively to the first offer may, and frequently does, backfire.

Exiting your business is a process, not an event, and time spent planning and marketing your sale will be rewarded. It can help you profitably wait out a bad market and get your company to the top of its game. A two-to-three-year planning horizon is usually optimum, although myriad circumstances such as economic and sector conditions, interest rates, and banks' willingness to lend can effect the sale and its timing. A longer time horizon allows you to bring in the right experts to help put your entrepreneurial house in order, strengthen financials and management, monitor market conditions, and evaluate potential buyers. It also allows you the breathing room to discover which of your important values will shape your sale.

Those businesses that were built for future sales are at an advantage in this case. We have worked with several owners who started their business with an eye on a particular buyer or type of buyer. Their preferences drove many of their decisions, such as which market to pursue and which computer system to buy (Answer: one that would integrate with the buyer's).

In the rare best-case scenario, selling your business could take as little as four months. Generally, once you place your business on the market—which depends on how much you're willing to invest to make it more salable or valuable—it could take about a year to find a buyer and complete the deal. Some sales, however, might take two or three years if the process halts for any reason—for instance, disgruntled buyers or sellers leave the table, then return and resume negotiations. Perhaps market conditions, industry trends, or interest rates change, or an unexpected event erodes the value of the business, and time is needed to recuperate. We have seen almost every timeframe imaginable, with unexpected twists and turns of every sort. Our point is that you should plan for it taking longer than you think. To avoid a forced sale, you should anticipate every delay you can and a few you can't when setting your timelines. You also should assure you're positioned financially to wait until receiving the right offer.

All in all, a window of optimum opportunity can open and shut swiftly. We have seen deals go south when the market turned. Yet that time spent in self assessment and business preparation bore fruit years later when the winds changed. Once your business is prepared and profitable for the long haul, it should be relatively easy to sell when you decide to. Personal and business planning and preparation, no matter what the timeline, will serve you well for this "deal of a lifetime."

Are You *Ready To Sell?*

Are you ready to let go of "your baby"? Even if you are ready to leave your business, it is still the ending of something that has had a huge role and tremendous impact on your life. You are leaving your business, and going where? Having that destination picked out, the topic of the next chapter, will ease you through this rough emotional time by giving you insight into what should be the best future you can design.

Conclusion

Selling a business—which often also is a life's purpose and way of life—is more than a transaction, because owning a business is more than a job. You shouldn't underestimate your business's importance as a source of meaning as well as money. And just as running a life and a business simultaneously is complex, running these two *and* also a sale while designing your post-sale life is more so. Perhaps the reasons and timing are yours, that of your business, or of the market, but the process starts with you. As this book outlines, assessing yourself and your business sets the stage for the best outcome. A holistic vision and values-based approach is the most rewarding one. You need to understand yourself, your business, and your goals before starting the journey.

Once you have decided to sell, this book can help you map your new destination and the path and timing to get there. It cannot, however, take the place of expert advisors dedicated to you and your company. Understand that although you're the authority about your business, you may not be an authority in the process of selling it. It is an effort that, surprisingly to some, spans the spectrum of your roles, from being a business leader to your role as an individual and family member. Its impact can span generations as newfound wealth flows through your family. Your years of hard work deserve the maximum return on investment by putting the right team around you.

Bernie Goldhirsh, founder of *Inc. Magazine*, has an interesting perspective on an entrepreneur as "an artist using both sides of his brain...someone who has the soul of an artist, and his expression is business." You may think that is too poetic, but we do not. We have the greatest respect for anyone savvy enough, creative enough, and persistent enough to build a successful business. We believe selling it should be a rewarding experience on all levels.

Takeaway Lessons

- The sale of every business starts with having a reason to sell, and it needs to be a reason persuasive enough to take you away from the business that brings you so much more than an income.
- Understanding your reasons is crucial to selling your firm. Absent strong reasons to sell, you'll likely not have the motivation to complete the arduous selling process, and potential buyers, sensing your indecision, will not engage with you.
- If other owners are involved in your business, everyone must understand each other's motivations and align their expectations for the sale's outcome.
- Not every business is saleable in its present state. Deficiencies in the business or infirmities in markets may militate against a sale. But most problems can be rectified if you're willing to make needed investments in your firm, plan sufficiently, and position your firm for the outcome you seek.

For additional resources and tools, visit www.sellingyourbusinessformore.com

CHAPTER 2

Goals and Objectives for the Sale

Introduction

What result do you want from the sale of your business? What is it you have been working so hard all these years for? What do *you* see as the most important outcome for you, your business, your family, your employees, and other stakeholders? As we've said many times, your business is more than a source of income; it is a source of identity, self-esteem, structure, goals, and friendships. Transitioning away from it is a journey from the known to the unknown, and it should be treated with more than just a passing thought. What is your destination? What do you hope to achieve by selling? Who needs to be part of this planning process? Understanding your business, financial, and personal goals is crucial to your sale having a successful outcome.

Typically, however, business owners define their objectives only financially—getting the highest price with the lowest taxes at closing, or perhaps setting up a future income stream. A goal could be to sell a piece of your business or all of it. Or it could be to retain control and finance growth through recapitalization.

You do need to think long and hard when assessing your financial needs, risk tolerance, and many related matters. What are the needs of other stakeholders and family members? Are key stakeholders and family members on board with the idea of the business being sold? Is it important to cash out at closing, or would you consider keeping a small investment in the newly sold company? Everyone has a financial dream, and whether the market supports yours will be revealed over time.

Business owners have told us time and again that their goals are larger than money. Money is important to them, but it is not the only thing. Just as their business means more than money to them, so does its sale, but they struggle to explain what that meaning is and what their goals are. Clients we've worked with often define the sale of their business in terms of money because they haven't taken time to think more broadly or don't know how. You should consider the larger and more holistic picture: the best-case picture of your future—work, family, activities, charities, adventures, spiritual and community commitment—after the sale. Selling is, after all, an opportunity to redefine your life. What will the new you be? We'll outline helpful questions later in this chapter to lead you through this process of self-discovery.

You have many choices for your life after the sale, both inside the business and out of it. Continuing on with the business, for example, may be an attractive alternative financially and psychologically. Are you interested in a transitional consulting contract, staying on the board, or running the company as a division of a larger buyer for a few years? Do you expect to pursue another business opportunity, or are you departing the world of commerce entirely to reengage your experience, time, and talent in a new way with new meaning, perhaps with a nonprofit or family foundation?

Answers to these and similar questions will influence the type of buyer and transaction you seek, and those answers also become the groundwork for your selling strategy. A good place to start is by knowing your definition of success and knowing which personal strategy for life after sale meets it.

Defining Success and the Roadmap to It

While running a business and hurtling toward urgent short-term and long-term goals, or perhaps motivated by an urgent reason to sell, you may not take time to reflect deeply on personal goals. You may even be uncomfortable doing so, or don't know how to start. Defining your goals as only numbers misses the mark. Your goals should be larger than getting as much money up front now and having time to golf later. You need to draw a new map with new destinations, because that map will clarify whom to target as buyers, how to structure the deal, and how to time the sale.

It's important to recognize, as Studs Terkel says in *Working*, that work doesn't just give "daily bread" but also "daily meaning." Don't underestimate the importance of this to your future happiness. Your goals as an owner who's preparing to sell your business should align with finding your own new daily meaning. Your goals should be holistic and cover many facets of your life beyond the numbers. They should be many and multileveled and should fall into categories of financial, business, health and welfare, and life after the sale.

Life After the Sale

Many business owners and advisors focus intently on preparing the business for sale, but not preparing you, the business owner. To have a successful exit, you need an idea about where you're going, and prepare to fire yourself from the business. Many sellers are consumed simply by running their business, and then they add selling it atop the turmoil of their day job. Having the time, tools, or aptitude to design the next chapter of a satisfying and productive life may not be at the front of your mind amid the chaos of the moment. Yet, having a compelling vision of your future will help you to shape the nature of the sale, sustain you in getting through it, and end up achieving success as you define it. Business was for Estee Lauder "a magnificent obsession." If it is the same for you, as it is for many business owners, what will you replace it with? (see figure 2.1).

Even if they don't realize it, entrepreneurs, usually an action-oriented group, have to think through what they want and how to get it. Otherwise, the typical Type A personality business owner, whose identity and reason for being may disappear with the sale of their business, will receive a major shock to his or her system. We work not just to pay the bills, but to connect with others, create an identity and sense of purpose, and to matter. The need for all that doesn't disappear when you sell your business.

Your Exit Plan

Just as you doubtless wrote a business plan when you started your business, you should draft an exit plan before selling it. Starting with the end in mind, you should thoughtfully design your future and direct the sale of your business to make that future a reality. Many owners aren't willing to put their skills, relationships, and experience out to pasture in a traditional retirement after selling their business. As studies show, remaining active and engaged in purposeful ways serves to keep the brain and body fit.

Developing an inspiring vision of the future requires you to tackle compelling questions such as those listed below. As you go through them, keep in mind

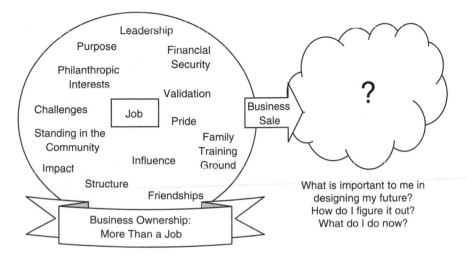

Figure 2.1 Business Ownership: More Than a Job

these words from Mark Twain: "Twenty years from now you will be more disappointed by the things that you didn't do than by the ones you did do. So throw off the bowlines. Sail away from the safe harbor. Catch the trade winds in your sails. Explore. Dream. Discover." And the discovery process starts by asking yourself questions such as:

- What does success mean to me now? What is most important to me in life? What values are important to me?
- How can I define my future life in accord with how I now define success and my values?
- What do I want my future life to look like—both day-to-day, and longer term? What changes must I make to achieve this?
- What have I enjoyed about my work and life and what do I want to continue with, and what to eliminate or disengage from?
- What other business ventures and jobs hold appeal to me? Can I begin to explore those now?
- How have my priorities changed over time, and what—and who—is important to me now?
- How can I best serve and enjoy my family? What activities do I want to share with them?
- What would I like to learn? Do? Where would I like to go? What dreams have been deferred to attend to my business? Is now the time to reignite them?
- What have I put off that needs my attention now? What needs less of my attention? What should I say "Yes" to, and what should I say "No" to?
- How do I want to be remembered and my life celebrated?

Keeping answers to these questions in mind, you should remember there are many paths to nirvana. Your path may be to stay on with your company, leave quickly, or remain in a role you and the buyer design. Once gone from the business, you can enter another, or perhaps you can move into a meaningful nonprofit role, choosing contribution over income. Another choice can be retirement to a life of leisure, which nonetheless you need to think through to decide how your time will be spent. Perhaps you should set aside time to decide the next option. Taking a break to rest, reset, and explore alternatives before defining the next chapter of your life can be very attractive.

Looking at your answers, sketch out at a high level the money needed to make these things happen. This becomes part of your financial requirements for life after the sale. If you choose a role inside your company or out where you will be making money through work or business-related income such as real estate, approximate what that inflow will be. You are starting to breathe life into not just what your future life will look like, but how much money you will have to support it.

Stay or Go?

Before you decide to sell, you should decide whether to stay with your company after you sell. There may be definite benefits to you and the buyer if you remain involved after closing. If you are financing the sale, you'll want to assure your investment is successful. Buyers, the business, and its stakeholders often benefit from such continuity, on-the-job training, and transfer of knowledge and relationships. Your remaining for a time also may have economic and psychological advantages for your transition and the new owner's transition into new roles.

Traditionally, sellers remain with their business past any transition period in one of three capacities: they become a consultant to the company and to the new owner, run the business for the buyer or as part of a buyer's larger organization, or take a seat on the buyer's board. The benefit to sellers is that they continue to contribute to the well-being of the company and its stakeholders. The new owner benefits from the seller's presence by learning more, faster, with less risk, and by transitioning key relationships more easily. Although each of these new roles requires some adjustments from everyone, each provides the former business owner with the opportunity to forge a post-sale life gradually. Of course, continuing with the business is not without its risk, as the following example from our experience illustrates.

Three partners had built a valuable company over time, and two of them had already decreased their work with the business prior to deciding to sell it. After the sale, they left the business entirely. The third partner, still working in the business full time, decided to stay with the company after it was sold. Unfortunately, a technical glitch caused the business to lose a valuable long-standing client. Management should have been imposing tighter controls on the issue all along, but the inevitable problem happened under the third partner's stewardship. He took it very hard and very personally. Loss of the client damaged the business financially and the third partner emotionally. He became withdrawn and eventually had to be replaced.

Our point? He could have left on a high note, one that would have given him a totally different experience and feeling about his life's work. Don't disregard the lesson and the questions that arise from it. How much do you really want to be responsible for your business after the sale? Should you hand the keys over now and take a victory lap, or risk financial and personal losses?

Go Where?

The "game" of business is a fascinating one that you may find difficult to leave. If your goal is to depart your company but stay in the business world, you should set aside time to explore starting a new business, buying a business, or landing a job at an existing firm. Many former owners are eager to find the next business puzzle to solve and an opportunity to reengage in the business arena. Others consider joining boards in the for-profit and nonprofit world. Choosing any of those alternatives would allow you to contribute your skills and network in a meaningful way without necessarily a full-time commitment.

Nonprofits hold a particular appeal for former business owners in that they allow you to pursue meaning over money. They may offer you the chance to reengage in a dream deferred, such as working for a cause that is important to you while being appreciated for the talent you bring. For yet other former business owners, selling the business represents an opportunity to choose impact over income by starting their own charities or becoming active philanthropists.

A "Gap Year"

Perhaps a "gap year" should be part of your plan. This is the European and increasingly American college student concept of taking time off for personal discovery during college or before starting a career. Running and selling a business are exhausting, and a pause to rest, have fun, and explore could be a wise use of your time. A restorative and contemplative sabbatical might reward you with the chance to study your next moves before enacting them.

Our advice to you is that it's best to put structure around your discovery process. We have recommended putting a flexible time limit—a year, for example—on the endeavor. On a more day-to-day level, consider dedicating one-third of the time on activities you've put off, one-third on maintaining or building your health, and one-third on actively searching for your personal "next big thing." Perhaps that means taking classes or meeting people, maybe engaging a personal coach, or taking up other activities that help you to assess yourself and find new ways to contribute and challenge yourself. Our clients have told us that this approach of thirds gives them a balanced break yet also pushes them to define the next phase of life.

Traditional Retirement?

If you're focused on a traditional notion of complete retirement without day-to-day obligations, you're wise to plan that out, too. Mapping the activities, courses, books, and people you want to engage can help you focus on your personal prize during the difficult process of selling your business. "Know thyself" becomes an operating principle here. As a business owner, you likely have been charging hard at goals all your life. Will you feel fulfilled without one ahead of you? For some, the concept of an endless vacation as a leisure-pursuing aristocrat looses luster after a while. To go from a hundred miles per hour to zero can seem attractive, but, over time, it may become unpalatable to a former boss who's accustomed to making things happen. Even in complete retirement, consider our advice of dividing life into thirds: catch up on things you have put off, improve your health, and find something challenging to devote energies to that makes you happy.

There's another, equally serious reason to envision your post-sale life earnestly before selling. Absent a vision of life after the sale, your uncertainty could be so disconcerting that it creates resistance to selling. Potential buyers who sense a seller's reluctance often back out of the sale, fearing it won't go smoothly or will stop mid-stride. Without investing time in parsing out what's important to you and designing an exciting future, you may resist engaging in the selling process or focus only on the money when more fulfilling options or potential buyers may be a better fit for your long term happiness.

Financial Goals

Having fully-developed goals for life after your business is sold helps you to set your timing and financial requirements for the sale. It is not, of course, that you set the price according to what you need for the lifestyle you want. But once you do get the initial business valuation, you can begin to make decisions on both a personal and professional level. If the business is worth less than you had hoped, you can decide on how to bring the valuation up and see if you have the time to do so. Overall, your goals will guide decisions about your selling price and time-frame, taking cash at closing, establishing how long you should stay involved with the business and in what role, whether to sell all of your business or retain a part, and whether your firm's real estate is to be included in the sale or is to be leased to the new owner. Steps in selling your business should include exploring your financial needs for the post-sale life you've envisioned, including the needs of other stakeholders, and related considerations, such as liquidity, timing, and risk tolerance.

As you ponder these issues broadly, understand your current financial require-ments and think through whether you want to maintain, improve, or simplify the lifestyle you have now. Tally up what you spend now, and then review your requirements going forward. Doing so will return your thoughts to what you value. If that's adventure, for instance, estimate what that dream trip around the world will cost. If it's education, perhaps you should estimate your own tuition or think about charitable strategies to help others attend college. If you value business achievement, consider redeploying your entrepreneurial talents by starting another business, buying one, or even investing in others as a micro-financier. How much money would you need?

This preliminary financial review sets the stage for proactive wealth transfer planning. Selling your business is a rare opportunity for liquid wealth. Tax, trust, gift, and estate planning should begin well before the transaction and should be based on your values as well.

Our process to this point has been at a high level to define your values and goals, design your future life, decide if you want to maintain, improve, or simplify your current lifestyle, and map out the income you will need to support it. Whatever life you are designing for yourself, do the math. Then think about how selling your business could support your life's expectations.

Business Health and Welfare Goals

Business owners have passionately invested their time, money, and heart into assembling and leading employees and navigating issues and obstacles to make their businesses successful. Thus, your vision of your post-sale life also will include your company's continuing health and welfare. For example, the goal for your sale could be to grow it by bringing in fresh management, diversifying the business, increasing market share, or injecting capital.

After so many hard years building a company, do you have strong preferences about the characteristics of the buyer to whom you sell, or a desire to keep the business intact after the sale? You may define the ideal buyer as one who shares your philosophy and approach to people, the company, and the community. If so, you may want to insist on a buyer who guarantees to retain your management team, promises to lock in employee benefits, or continues to support the same charities your business did. Is it critical to sell your firm to someone who shares your commitment to the environment, or to a particular location so employees do not have to move? These are a few of the issues involving your business's health and welfare that you'll want to consider alongside your own, and will impact whom you target to sell it.

Putting It All Together

This process of defining your personal and professional goals, as well as goals for your business, will influence many aspects of your sale. Therefore, it's absolutely essential that you consider them thoroughly and thoughtfully. To clarify your thinking, consider consulting an outside advisor—someone experienced in guiding your process of discovery and shaping your vision for sale of your business, your departure from it, and your post-sale plans. The end you hold in mind will guide every decision you make to enhance your business prior to sale, design your optimal sale, and choose the right buyer.

Financial, business, and personal goals then flow into how you decide to sell your business and to whom. An additional significant ingredient in your exit recipe is your risk tolerance. A conservative seller might target a full-cash sale. One willing to share some risk and rewards of the business going forward might consider, for example, selling 80 percent of the value of the business and retaining an interest in it for several years afterward. These and a variety of other options are driven by how much risk you're comfortable with.

Given these considerations and many others, your goals for a sale could include:

- Obtaining the highest after-tax proceeds
- Paying minimal taxes
- Securing the best long-term growth opportunity for your business
- Keeping your business as a separate company or merging with another
- Getting all cash at the closing, or locking in a long-term income stream
- Holding a job with the new owner, perhaps earning a percentage of the profit
- Staying involved in the business as a director, consultant, or operator of a subsidiary
- Setting a time frame for closing the deal
- Selling all of the business, or keeping a piece of it
- Retaining ownership of your company's real estate or realizing lease income
- Maintaining family harmony
- Assuring a continued role for family members and valued employees
- Keeping your management team or employees and their benefits intact

Whatever post-sale goals you set, you cannot relax once you've decided to sell your enterprise. You must remain engaged and committed to continuing the success of your business, and not just be content with the selling process or the allure of new endeavors after your business is sold. A business is a provider not just for the owner but also for employees. To lose focus could reduce the value and price of your business and devastate employees who made your business the success it has become.

Conclusion

Values are everything we hold important. Caring for family and employees, having financial freedom, serving others, contributing to charity, and preserving the environment may be on your list of personal values. You shouldn't gloss over them and go directly for the money. Success is broader than that, and after all the hard work you have put into the business, you owe it to yourself to understand what is important to you and how selling the business can help make that a reality. According to Dr. Larry Jost of the University of Cincinnati, "Your values can pull you in different directions. The only people who claim value questions are easy are those who don't think for themselves."

What direction will you be pulled in? How can selling your business get you there? On a professional level, for example, your value of caring for people could impact the selling process as you choose to target companies that would keep jobs intact for your employees. We recommend you ask these hard questions of yourself and understand that the process of selling your business should be shaped and guided by a definition of success that includes what you find personally, as well as professionally, important.

Takeaway Lessons

- Having a successful sale means defining what "success" means for you financially and personally and for the continuation of your business. You need to establish that definition at the start of the selling process and let it guide you at each step toward conclusion.
- At the start of your sale, you need to determine whether you prefer to remain with your firm or leave, and, if so, at what point after the transaction closes. Making the first determination requires that you have a vision of your life after selling and a roadmap to follow when you look ahead. Making the second requires you to have a responsible exit plan and a destination.
- Your future financial needs and tolerance for risk also play in the decision you make. Whether you opt for a traditional retirement or a career change to new business and charitable ventures, you'll need to ensure you have the income you need. You also will need to decide what degree of risk you can accept for the goals you've set. The value of the business, not what you need financially, is the basis of the selling price. However what you need will impact how you invest in your business to bring the value up, the payment structure of the deal you agree to, and timing the sale.
- Your business moves into the future without you, but your vision for the business goes with it. You will want to know a potential buyer shares that vision, whether it's for continuing your business's civic prominence, making the investment to carry the business to new heights, or maintaining the employment and benefits of your employees.

For additional resources and tools, visit www.sellingyourbusinessformore.com

CHAPTER 3

Managing People and Processes During Change

Introduction

Change—the entire process of selling your business is about change. Its quantity and degree depend on many factors: complexity and size of your business, the deal structure, your preparation, how dependent your business is on you, and many more. Like many owners selling their business, you may misunderstand and underestimate the impact of this change on others. William Bridges, author of *Managing Transitions,* put it best:

> Before you begin something new, you have to end what used to be.... Before you can become a different kind of person, you must let go of your old identity. So beginnings depend on endings. The problem is, people don't like endings. Yet change and endings go hand in hand: change causes transition, and transition starts with an ending. If things change within an organization, at least some of the employees and managers are going to have to let go of something. It isn't the changes themselves that the people in these cases resist. It's the losses and endings that they have experienced and the transition that they are resisting.

Regardless of your firm's size, you and your management team must guide people past their resistance and through a series of changes that, to them, are also losses. You need a process to help you anticipate what lies ahead, with experienced advisors pointing out opportunities and pitfalls. In all cases, you need to understand that sale of your business brings significant changes that people around you may see as threatening.

Some practitioners believe transition planning and communication planning belong later in the sequence of selling and buying a business. Our experience has taught us otherwise. In this chapter we will review the process at a high level, and recommend a thoughtful and decisive inclusion of these topics early in your planning. As soon as you've decided to sell, it's critical to understand the changes involved and discuss how and when you will pass the torch to the new owners. Communicating to internal and external stakeholders correctly is essential. Finally, a properly conceived selling process has a contingency plan for identifying and mitigating risks of many types.

Process Overview

Once you've identified your values and goals and decided to sell your business, the selling process unfolds in three stages:

- Planning and preparation—this book will outline many actions you can take to improve your business along with actions necessary to the deal.
- Marketing and negotiation—finding and approaching qualified buyers, responding to bids, and negotiating the best deal.
- Managing the transaction and transition—completing contracts, closing the deal, and transitioning to the new normal.

Selling your business is a complex, time-consuming project, and it's likely the most important one of your business life. Although you won't do all of the detailed work, you must work personally with all external and internal teams. You need to guide their actions in the context of your selling plan and to document goals and track each element of them to completion. Since this is probably the most important professional and financial event of your career, letting it get out of control is not an option.

Sellers and buyers must understand and respect the sophistication and impact of the effort. "Habit is habit," Mark Twain said, "and not to be flung out the window by any man, but coaxed downstairs a step at a time." Your people will need your coaxing, because selling a business can disrupt everyone's work and relationship "habits." Leading people through change takes time, and it's a struggle to insert a threatening happening and new work into the regular stream of activities and habits that consume their business day.

Besides changes that happen *because* you're selling the business, the *process* of selling it represents change. Selling a business—a new experience for many—is a full-time activity placed upon people who already have full-time jobs. You have to be careful not to kill the goose that's laying your golden eggs. Overtaxing people with work or anxiety about their jobs will decrease their productivity. Managing the process correctly, as with any sophisticated project, is paramount, even if your business is a small one. It's essential to have detailed project plans that identify resources and time frames specifically. Most businesses have not been through the selling process before and lack methodologies, tools, or institutional skills to draw upon. Calling on experienced advisors will help to forge realistic plans and expectations and bring the support you will need.

As a hard-charging entrepreneur, your first reaction may be that we are exaggerating the issue and attempting to pamper the employees. Not true. Our experience has shown us that paying attention to the people side of the equation always pays off.

Project Management: Getting the Right Things Done

According to Dr. Warren Bennis, leadership is the capacity to translate vision into reality. You have the vision of selling your company, and now are planning to translate it into reality. This is not a trivial task. Throughout the process of selling your business, your future and the future of your business are at stake. In a later chapter, we discuss assembling the teams of experts you will need to make the best future a reality. Once you have assembled those strong internal and external teams, you will work alongside them to shape and monitor project processes, problems, people, and strategic alignment. You will oversee the creation of a project plan that outlines tasks, milestones, dependencies, and deliverables, just as you would with any significant strategic initiative. Doing so may be more fun than planning to do so, but execution cannot be a seat-of-the-pants endeavor. As management gurus Bassidy, Charan, and Burck in their book *Execution* point out, "unless you translate big thoughts into concrete steps for action, they're pointless."

When reviewing your project plan, assure that goals and priorities are set and deliverables are tied to established dates. It's customary to hold weekly meetings to track the advance of the selling process. These meetings will be small, for the initial team will have few members. Establish the discipline of weekly meeting early in your selling process. It will be helpful throughout the entire process as your efforts multiply and the number of team members grow.

A Few Pointers

While you are putting the plan together, assure you schedule first those projects and activities having the greatest immediate influence on the valuation and readiness of your business for sale. For one thing, qualified buyers appear sooner than expected. For another, as we're fond of saying to our clients: tough stuff first. Get it out of the way and move to the next prioritized item.

Determine that all tasks are assigned proper resources, that everyone receives needed support, and that essential resources are not overbooked. Teams tend to over-rely on a few accomplished internal experts, spreading their energies and expertise too thinly. In our planning sessions with clients, we have teams take separate projects and create plans independently. When we bring them together and review their plans as a group, there are inevitably a few central people that everyone is counting on at the same time. This is a genuine vulnerability, not just a dependency. Training, support, or outside resources may be the solution in these situations. Be alert to the need for them.

Another frequent problem is failing to build buffer time into the schedule. Unexpected interruptions and unanticipated tasks are inevitable; therefore, our experience has shown that adding 15 percent to the expected time frame is wise. Three aspects of the process and project planning are frequently overlooked or undervalued: ownership transfer, communications planning, and contingency planning. To avoid that deficiency in your thinking and executing your selling process, let's examine each.

Ownership Transfer and Transition Planning

As mentioned earlier, you may intend to stay with the company for a time after the sale, or you may intend to leave quickly. Either way, you are trying to find a way to fire yourself that makes the most sense for you and selling the business. Often, sellers remain with the business a year or so after the sale, although the amount of time depends on their goals and those of the new owners, the complexity of the business, and the type of sale and financing. Earn-out scenarios frequently are longer than one year. In any case, your plan for selling the business and transferring ownership must specify when and how you depart, and it must be agreed to by the buyer.

You also need to protect your ability to earn a living after the sale. In the chapter dealing with contracts in depth, the noncompete agreement will be reviewed.

Compared to the date you plan to depart, the actual date may surprise you. We were recently exposed to a situation in which the seller doubted he could work for a private equity owner. Therefore, he set a twelve-month horizon for leaving the business. However, the company did well, the relationship was great, the business thrived, and the seller ended up staying four years, to everyone's satisfaction. We know of other instances where the agreement was for two years, and both parties agreed to separate amicably after one year because all contractual obligations were met. Nonetheless, these are exceptions to what we've found to be generally true.

Passing the Torch

Once you've completed your sale, you face what might be the most emotionally difficult duty in any career: passing the torch. Knowing they must eventually step down and relinquish the crown, some business owners delay starting the selling process longer than they should. While at times exhausting and frustrating, leadership is also rewarding. It is good to be king in your own kingdom. Earning respect, exercising influence, and creating jobs are worthy and wonderful endeavors. Business owners take pride in having a generational impact on employees, an industry, and a community. Unfortunately, some owners make themselves the center of too many decisions and activities. Not only does that make their business unhealthily dependent on them, but it also makes the thought of leaving it a shock for the owner and employees. Overcoming that shock is essential for the transition of ownership. Relinquishing a torch held so long can be wrenching, but transition planning helps to make transfer of ownership real and smooth, psychologically and operationally.

Transition planning deals with everything involved in transferring responsibilities. It starts with you, the soon-to-be former owner, thinking through what must happen strategically and tactically. Especially, you must outline relationships and responsibilities to be transitioned. As discussed in a later chapter, this may entail developing a stronger second tier of management by delegating decision-making and by investing in professional development—both on the job and management training programs.

Dates and Notes

Capture your key actions and dates in the sale contract, and keep notes about what you do, how you do it, and how best to ease responsibilities onto the proper successor. Although this seems an administrative bother, your notes can be invaluable in capturing nuances of running your company. We know of one company that assigned the CEO an administrative assistant specifically dedicated to staying by his side to chronicle what he was doing and how he made decisions.

Be sure to integrate important dates into the communication plan discussed in the following section. Determine who needs to know when you are leaving and who has taken over responsibilities. A communications plan as discussed below will assure this is properly communicated. Your purpose is to meet all contractual commitments within a declared time in a way that reflects your goals, the new owner's goals, and those of the business. And you want to make sure these changes are known appropriately.

A signed contract in hand, you and the new owner should build on preliminary transition work you completed earlier. Together, you should chalk out a properly constructed, detailed, and realistic timetable. This formal, written timetable should stipulate when transfer of ownership is complete, when day-to-day responsibilities shift over, and when you depart. As these details are defined, you can begin to think through the impact the change of ownership will have on others. It also should include important metrics—for instance, earn-outs agreed to in the sale contract.

When reviewing metrics such as earn-outs, assure they do not set you and the new owner at cross-purposes. We recently were involved in a fairly common situation in which earn-out metrics became a source of conflict. The seller's earn-out was based on business growth and profitability. The buyer, after acquiring the company to integrate it into a larger one, wanted to install new computer systems. He also wanted to charge the former business owner for the systems, dedicate some of the former business owner's staff to making them work, and take people out of the field for training. The seller saw the expense and diversion of staff as a threat to his earn-out, and he began working against the buyer on it and other initiatives. Spell it out upfront and you will avoid such issues.

Effecting the Transition

Your business transition is complete when you formally hand ownership over to the new owner, who assumes total responsibility for the business. You may be involved in an interim of training and transition before your business comes under the guidance of its new owner. We'll discuss in a later chapter the types of potential roles you might fill after the sale. Whatever that role is, if any, a sound transition plan helps you and the buyer attain stated goals. It also helps protect the viability of the business under new leadership.

No matter how long you remain with the business after sale, you should help ease the new owner into leadership in the way that best fits your situation. However difficult it may be for you to shift from making decisions to supporting a new decision maker, it's difficult for employees as well. You need to guide staff gently away from their previous and comfortable routine and their relationship with you and help people to accept leadership of the new owner. Be ever vigilant against undermining the new owner or sending conflicting messages. Consistently and persistently direct people to the new owner, even though it would have been faster and easier to handle a matter yourself.

Your office, as a symbol of leadership, should belong to the new owner as soon as possible. As minor as this may seem, we have seen it seriously obstructing more than one transition of leadership. The former owner may have been passive-aggressive, reluctant, or blind to the importance of handing over his office, but staying put sent absolutely the wrong message to employees and the new owner.

You and the new owner must agree how you will be available to the new owner and to employees, suppliers, vendors, and customers. There are many transitional intervals you can consider, and one of the best includes scheduling time off before returning to the business in a new capacity. Taking a vacation is a visible and psychological transition that breaks habits and solidifies the change.

Even so, there will come a point at which the new owner takes over and the two of you agree you can leave. It can be a momentous occasion to know you finally have met your commitments and goals and can move on. If your departure happens earlier than stipulated in the contract, your exit needs to be negotiated and documented. The new owner should formally attest that you have completed your contractual responsibilities and are free to depart. Otherwise, the new owner may later blame your early departure for the business not fulfilling expectations.

Announcing the Sale:
Change Management and Communication Planning

Immediately upon making your decision to sell, you must determine who needs to be told prior to the sale and who can be told after. A preliminary communication plan may seem complicated, but it simply means setting some time aside to think through who your stakeholders are, along with when, what, and how to tell them about your impending sale. You must inform key family members, for example, at the start.

The First to Know

One of your most difficult decisions is when to tell key employees about the pending change in ownership. You may justifiably fear that these crucial resources will leave the company or will tell competitors, customers, suppliers, or other employees. However, at some point in your selling process, you must tell them what's happening and why. You may need these important managers and associates to prepare information for the sale, and prospective buyers may want to interview them. And, once you've clued them in, you can coach them on how to position the company. Also, you'll want to start discussions with key employees early in the selling process if you will offer them "stay put" bonuses, as discussed later. If you leave them in the dark until the last minute, they may feel you have not treated them with respect. Their resentment may surface in unwanted ways toward you and or the buyer.

At the front end of the selling process, you should include only those who need to know in your communications. After the sale and after you and the buyer agree on transition roles and time frames, you still must work with the new owner to unfold your communications selectively. Change is difficult, and people may keep looking to you as the leader and decision maker if you're still involved with the business. After years as the authority figure, you may be similarly reluctant to give up the reins. Remember, you and your employees are feeling a sense of loss. Putting the transition process in place and communicating it fully can make this change a psychological, organizational, and operational reality. Getting it right is crucial for your successful exit and for the new owner's authority within the firm. It sets the tone and pace for the change.

What exactly is the change we're talking about? At several points earlier in this chapter, we laid out a phased approach to understanding the impact of ownership change. Prior to the sale, we advocated keeping notes and paying attention to what you are doing tactically and strategically, so you can begin to understand how to transfer your business responsibilities and relationships. This is also an opportunity to assess and build the management team needed to handle responsibilities you will give them. After the deal is closed, we recommended that you and the new business owner map out the transfer of responsibilities, taking your presale notes to a more detailed level of assigning dates and resources for the transfer.

Assess the Change

Up to this point you have been documenting what the changes are, but not their impact. Now is the time to assess the impact of change for both employees and the new owner. Moving Task A to John Jones, for example, will affect other people, processes, and systems. It could mean changing how some of your direct reports work with him, what computer systems he will need access to, and what training he will need. Further, you need to document any tasks he must hand over to his replacement, and make these same determinations about her as the new manager. Each of these changes, at the very least, requires coordinated communications. People will need to know to deal with him on Task A, the computer staff will need to give him access to the pertinent system, and Jane Smith will need to be informed of the change and trained for her new responsibilities.

So the first step in forming your transition plan is to understand the impact of the ownership change and the differing needs for internal and external communication that this will drive. Different constituencies will have different concerns and will need them to be addressed. As in the example above, employees will be affected in varying ways. Some may be asked to relocate, change responsibilities and reporting structure, or leave the company. High-level clients, suppliers, and other outside stakeholders also will need to be guided into productive and positive relationships with the new owner. The industry and community must be informed in a way that makes sense for you and them. And you and the new owner must work in concert on each communication.

Overall, the selling process requires you to anticipate and understand what changes are likely and to communicate them appropriately. You should build on your previous work with a simple change assessment and stakeholder analysis. This may sound cumbersome, complicated, or unnecessary in a smaller company, but it merely documents what changes are likely and whom they affect. It's intended to gauge the impact of changes large or small on disparate groups of stakeholders. It becomes the basis of the communications plan. Once you map changes and their effects, you can determine the appropriate messages and media to deliver them.

In larger organizations your change assessment might produce an extensive document. This is particularly true for mergers, as discussed in a later chapter. But for organizations of any size a thoughtful review of changes is necessary. Even a simple ownership transfer should not ignore a change assessment. Transferring ownership may seem straightforward—old boss out, new boss in—but employees, suppliers, and customers don't know how they will be affected by the sale, and their uncertainty could attenuate productivity or vital relationships. Keep in mind it would be counterproductive if you promised during the sale to take care of your employees, and excluded them from the loop during a time they feel loss and uncertainty. You and the incoming owner can mitigate these consequences with a plan for clear communication about the process and its impact.

Spreading the Word

At this point you have documented potential changes and whom they impact. The next steps are determining whom to tell what, when, and how. You need to shape appropriate messages with the new owner to reflect your reasons for selling, your values, and their future. Information needs to be delivered to stakeholders in effective formats and frequency. You should tell the story in a respectful, logical, meaningful way. You should respect the hierarchy within your organization and use it to guide your timing, method, and message. Whether you provide information via a personal call, a letter, or a press release will be driven by that hierarchy. The tool to do this is a communications plan.

A comprehensive communication plan consolidates the information you have been collecting to date, and, working with the new owner, puts it in action form. It is the tool that helps you determine how to communicate relevant information efficiently and effectively to constituents in supporting the successful transfer of business ownership. It guides the development of appropriate messages and identifies media to deliver them.

For example, a customary way to announce your sale is by convening an all-hands meeting with employees. It's recommended that you, the seller, open the meeting, announce the sale and reasons for it, and give important dates for the unfolding process and your departure. You should introduce the buyer and show confidence in his or her experience. The buyer might then preside over the meeting to become recognizable by employees and to symbolize the larger transition under way. The buyer usually explains his or her reasons for buying the business and presents any plans that are appropriate—without discussing the deal's terms. In a merger scenario, employees will be eager to understand how the two companies will integrate and how that will impact them.

A not uncommon scenario in companies large and small is news about the pending sale leaking out. Secrets may be harder to keep in smaller, close-knit companies where everyone feels like family and finds it difficult to keep such important news confidential. There are several ways to handle this. The first is to anticipate it, highlighted by the owner of a Public Relations firm in our Afterword. He told his employees up front that he was going to sell the company, and that he would take care of them. He kept them informed throughout the process and did indeed take care of them. This set the employees and new owner up for success. If the sales process has already begun, you could acknowledge that a sale is under consideration, and that business owners frequently consider selling the business and nothing has been finalized yet. A third approach is to deny everything. In such a case, when the sale is announced, however, your credibility is damaged, and resentment and resistance may begin brewing.

We highly recommend waiting until the deal is complete before you and the new owner inform external business colleagues. As set out in the communication plan and decided between you and the buyer, the announcement should be swift and strategic, yet respectful of each stakeholders' importance. Obviously, stakeholders who represent the firm's most important relationships should hear the news first and from you, not from a competitor or industry publication. For other stakeholders, your phone call, letter, or an e-mail with an attached fact sheet or press release may be appropriate. It should be succinct and confidence-boosting and include the same information conveyed to employees and business associates: what's happening and why, important dates, and what is and isn't expected to change. The press release should go to all appropriate media outlets.

This is an opportunity to reinforce your values and your company's brand. Like politicians who stay "on message," so, too, must you and the new owner. Both must agree about what the right messages are and determine your separate roles in delivering them. Both of you should align your messages with the overall goals of the sale and the business's brand.

Contingency Planning

Notwithstanding your best planning, execution, and communication before, during, and after the transition, some employees inevitably believe they will not fit well with the new owner and situation. Don't assume their ongoing loyalty to the business. Unfortunately, business owners seldom appreciate fully the consequences of personnel leaving. Ironically, they insist on recovery plans against losing technology, facilities, or equipment, but they don't take the same precautions to protect against losing people. Therefore, you should anticipate which critical operations would be disrupted by losing personnel. If someone critical to the operation of your business left during the selling process, would it noticeably disrupt your business or even the sale? You should document essential processes, including the activities, personnel, and equipment associated with them.

As we'll cover in the next chapter devoted to preparing your business for sale, you need to determine which processes deserve your first attention when forming a contingency plan. The guideline is simple: consider which processes are important in generating revenue and which bring greatest value to clients. Is the activity a core competency or a marketplace differentiator? Also consider which processes consistently have problems and which rely too heavily on too few people to resolve. Look for congruency of a critical process with a few irreplaceable resources, and begin contingency planning there. We know of a situation within a small printing company where everyone on the shop floor was cross-training on all presses. A smart move whether being sold or not, it prevents an issue surfacing during the selling process and potentially damaging the process.

Conclusion

Even detailed project plans and raw data, however, will not reveal the whole story. You need to take a big step back and assess your organization's capacity for change. You should be asking questions like the following to help uncover issues and resolve them swiftly:

- What are my biggest challenges confronting the sale and transition and why?

- What can my organization do about these challenges now?
- Historically, how successful has my organization been at managing projects and implementing change?
- If success has been limited, what will be different this time?

Selling the business means assessing it honestly and beyond merely considering the numbers. Actively understanding and addressing the capacity to change is a vital element of success.

As Dr. Bridges pointed out, new beginnings are dependent on endings, and these endings can be hard for many people to work through. Although you will be transitioning business ownership to someone else, people still will look to you for help in dealing with their loss and to understand how they fit in the new scenario. By taking time to understand how to deal with change and manage the selling process, you are investing in the future of the business. Planning for your transition and communicating it wisely will help assure that all will go as smoothly as it can.

Takeaway Lessons

- Selling a business is entirely about change, and change is both an ending and a beginning. It is a process and a time period filled with opportunity, but also anxiety and resistance. You should respect the impact a sale can have on a business and its employees.
- The three-part selling process is complicated and requires strong internal and external teams that are properly staffed and provided with the necessary resources.
- You likely need to make investments in your business and modifications to your operations before bringing your firm to market. Your first priority in doing so should be to decide which enhancements will add revenues and improve customer satisfaction.
- At each step in the selling process, you must consider what steps are necessary for an effective transition to a new owner. Those steps will include documenting your processes and operations, assessing who is affected by the sale and how, and communicating internally and externally.
- You must anticipate every possible contingency and continually monitor the progress of your sale and the effect it is having. You and your firm's new owner need to agree on the supportive and advisory role you will play, and you need to display support for the new owner honestly and consistently. And remember: the day will come when you must relinquish the reins.

For additional resources and tools, visit www.sellingyourbusinessformore.com

CHAPTER 4

Preparing Your Company for Sale

Introduction

Selling your business can be a sprint or a marathon, depending on your motivations and time frames for selling and the receptivity of the marketplace. Owners sprinting for the exit can still benefit from improvements to their businesses that may increase their selling price. Those with a marathon journey—looking to sell in two to three years—can invest more time and reap greater rewards. It's a matter of weighing benefits, time, resources, and, perhaps most important, will. There are actions you can take now to increase the value of your business when you offer it for sale no matter what your timeline.

This chapter details steps to evaluate your business as a buyer would, and improve business profitability and solidify transfer of ownership based on what is your top priority for increasing the price quickly. Steps include strengthening your bottom-line performance, getting finances in order, addressing known problems, emphasizing strategies and business lines attractive to the buyer market, and putting a strong management team in place. Your staff may ask why these efforts are taking place sooner than you're willing to disclose why, so it's best to couch them as merely competitiveness and profitability initiatives, and leave it at that.

Bringing experienced advisors on board early in the process will pay dividends here. We have been brought in as early as three years before a sale to uncover the values and goals of the owner and to advise about positive, value-enhancing opportunities that strengthen the business and negative issues that need correcting. This proactive planning and prioritized execution of changes have given the business owner a tremendous boost in achieving his sale on his terms. Diversifying a customer base, cleaning up pending litigation, and rectifying known issues as well as dozens of other ways to improve the business take time. And you have a business to run.

Beware of shortcuts. We know of advisors who have recommended imme-diately cutting all research and development costs and laying off people in an attempt to improve cash flow quickly. These ploys, however, can be transparent, and sophisticated buyers will view them as discrediting. Always take a thought-ful and judicious approach. Your guiding principle should be "What's bad for the business is bad for the valuation of the business."

When preparing your firm for sale, you should weigh all investments of money, energy, and time for their likelihood of providing a high and fast return and of positioning you to act quickly if a buyer appears immediately. Regard this chapter as a guide to understanding what can be done, and for prioritizing projects and actions.

Preparing for Sale

Once you've decided to sell, create a plan for making your business more valu-able, less risky, and more attractive as the buyer would see it. Initiatives could involve one or two large projects, but they most likely will be a group or portfo-lio of smaller, prioritized ones—a series of sprints you can execute as the sale's time horizon permits. Your goal is to situate your business to attract the largest group of potential buyers in the shortest amount of time.

Shaping your action plan also forces you to change your personal perspective. By thinking about preparing your business for sale, you also begin separating your personal future from that of your business. Although you, like most owners starting the selling process, may feel your business is in your DNA, you'll even-tually see a personal and professional future that's separate and productive.

Prepare a Preliminary Business Valuation

A recommended first step in preparing to sell is to conduct a preliminary business valuation. A preliminary valuation benchmarks your estimate of your firm's value against a range of recent selling prices. It highlights features that make your firm more valuable to buyers, thereby intimating which of your contemplated enhance-ments will most improve its selling price. It also helps you to calculate return on investments you make to improve your company prior to sale. And finally, it helps you to understand what range of prices you can realistically expect. If a competitor has recently been purchased by a strategic buyer for a high price, that precedent may inflate your expectations. Or you may be pleasantly surprised at the high number. Whichever way it turns out, it's best to have your feet grounded firmly in reality and begin to form a plan to improve the business's value.

Have a Formal Business Plan

Update your existing business plan—or create one if none exists. Although many businesses call their annual budget a "business plan," it isn't what we are talking about here. A business plan is a written document that management follows to develop, grow, and manage a business. Business plans address strategic and operational issues. They describe your organization's present status and plans for the future, and they map financial, operational, and marketing strategies that enable a business to reach its goals. This would be a good time to revisit your mission or vision statement as well. Does it capture your business principles and goals? Does it send the message that is both congruent with what your organization does and that will attract the buyer you want? If you've never created a business plan, believe it or not, now is a great time to pull one together. You may find that you have an opportunity to increase the value of your company in a relatively short time—or you may discover something of hidden value that will help your sale price.

Besides providing strategic information in prepping your business for sale, your business plan becomes part of your marketing package when you sell. It should include three years of audited financials and a three-year financial projection, as that's what buyers usually request. Also, summarize your industry and its growth trends and include a review of competitors and how your business is positioned against them. A buyer will want to understand the size and health of your industry.

This is a chance to put into place plans to address particular challenges your company faces. For example, if your industry has growth challenges due to global competition, look for both the healthiest areas of the industry and business and focus building around them, or create new capabilities to address the stressed industry circumstances. These would then be documented in the business plan.

An objective SWOT analysis (strengths, weaknesses, opportunities, and threats) is a standard element of a business plan (figure 4.1). Although it may

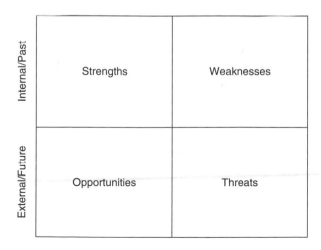

Figure 4.1   SWOT Matrix

be difficult for you to be objective—you'll be inclined to overstate strengths and downplay weaknesses—an honest discussion about weaknesses makes you a more credible seller. In addition, you may have legal and moral obligations to disclose certain relevant facts to potential buyers. Hiring an advisor or consultant might keep you objective and move your preparation for sale more swiftly, because a thorough and objective SWOT analysis helps buyers determine what future investment they need to make. Credibility will be enhanced by the inclusion of any third-party industry reports, analyses, forecasts, and similar documents. Investment bankers can be useful in the preparation stage by providing substance to the information memorandum. Business consultants and investment bankers also can work with you and your management to develop a business plan.

Put Strong Talent on Your Board of Directors

A stellar board of directors can enhance the performance of a business as well as its reputation and identity. Generally, corporations are required by state law to have a board of directors, while partnerships and limited liability companies may elect to establish a board of directors in their partnership or operating agreements. If your company has a board of directors, you should periodically evaluate the board's composition and qualifications in light of the firm's overall business objectives. Examine your current board and decide if all of its members contribute significantly or if bringing aboard new members would serve your business or bring desirable experience to a potential sale process. Remember that it can take time to change an existing board, given that valuable and in-demand people can take time to connect with and will need to familiarize themselves with your company before making a decision to join your board.

Evaluate current and prospective directors not solely for their contribution, but also consider how a buyer would view them. For example, a business looking to expand into international markets might bring aboard directors with relevant experience or an academic expert in the field. The board could be comprised of family members who have professional credentials and members inside and outside of the firm. In a private company, it's acceptable and expected that family members and insiders will dominate, but expert outside board members can bring significant insights and useful networks that potential buyers will value.

Your selling effort should include your board, especially since they and company shareholders will approve the final deal. You could involve the chairman, certain directors, or set up a special committee to be an objective resource for evaluating various alternatives and buyers.

Strengthen Your Management Team

Ralph Nader said he "starts with the premise that the function of leadership is to produce more leaders, not more followers." This certainly is true when operating a business, and it's critical when selling a business. A strong management team is among the most important criteria for selling a business and for making it successful after the sale. Smaller businesses frequently fall into the trap of being too owner dependent. If that next tier team is not in place, creating it should be your top priority upon deciding to sell. Assess your team honestly, using a consultant if necessary, and determine how to bring their skills up to the level needed. This could include on-the-job training or professional development classes. If you decide to hire senior executives while planning your sale, you likely will contract with them for a payoff when the sale concludes. If you have a longer sale horizon, offer tax-advantaged incentives through equity or synthetic equity arrangements. Always consult a tax advisor about such matters.

The time to estimate this kind of endeavor is difficult. It depends on how ready your people are now to pick up additional responsibilities, how available relevant education is, and, if you choose to go outside the company, how accessible top talent is. This could take as long as two to three years.

Top business owners always develop and delegate authority to appropriate people. Initiating the sale process is an opportunity to see how your company can lessen reliance on you. As Theodore Roosevelt advised, the boss should have "sense enough to pick good men to do what he wants done, and the self restraint to keep from meddling with them while they do it."

Recast Financial Statements

Just as home-owners "stage" their house before putting them on the market, you'll want to dress up your business. You certainly try to improve its appearance physically, and you also should financially. Your accounting policies must follow accepted industry standards. Potential buyers will request audited financial statements showing income, expenses, and tax returns for the past three years. Tax computations must be current. If placing your business for sale in the middle of your fiscal year, prepare interim financial statements.

A potential buyer will ask who prepared your financial statements and will prefer the opinion of outside professional accountants over that of an internal CFO or controller. Any financing institution a buyer approaches also will require audited financial statements. Therefore, it is essential to prepare them early.

In preparing a business for sale, it's customary to recast historical financial statements so as better to display prospects of its future performance for a new owner. "Recasting" financials doesn't mean jiggering the books. Rather, it means acknowledging that you probably operated in a way that minimized taxes. For example, you may have awarded perks and benefits to yourself and to family members, accelerated depreciation, or reinvested profits in capital improvements. These kinds of actions benefitted your business—from a tax standpoint and otherwise—during your ownership, but they don't accurately portray your company's profitability and opportunity for a new owner. To portray your firm's actual potential, recast financial statements to remove their effects and adjust your income statement to present what would have been real, operational cash flow. For example, re-report your salary and family members' salary to approximate current market salary levels. Expenses such as intercompany rentals, travel and entertainment, and club dues are candidates for recasting. An accountant can help identify and resolve these matters, as can your investment banker, especially if your sale is imminent.

Before recasting financials, however, be aware that getting a history of clean financials may take several years, and that some buyers accept only original financials. You should have them available and be able to demonstrate adequate financial systems and controls.

Improve Financial Performance to Improve Selling Price

The buyer is naturally looking to see your company's financial health. While you're preparing and recasting, you may see that financial and performance ratios point toward ways to improve your business's performance and profitability. Act on what you discover. Whatever improves the financial health and performance of your business also improves its selling price.

Obsolete and Unproductive = Gone

While preparing your firm for sale is when you should take steps you perhaps should have taken long ago. For example, sell or scrap obsolete or slow-moving inventory. Compare product rework against industry averages and correct the causes of deficiencies. Divest unproductive assets that can't be sold. Write off receivables that are truly uncollectable. It may also be advisable to discontinue or remove unrelated businesses. For example, one of our recent clients ran a metal plating business that also owned a microbrewery. Although a brewery was fun hobby for our client, it would be difficult to find a buyer for a metal plating business who had a similar interest in owning a microbrewery. We advised him to sell the brewery to the current day-to-day manager, and it was a strong strategic move for both parties involved.

Your business and its selling price may benefit from analyzing profitability of product and service lines: what doesn't pay doesn't stay. External advisors and consultants can help to perform the analysis, and they may find other ways to increase profitability. Examples would be a determination of whether the market could support a price increase for your products or whether you could bundle them with others and raise prices on the total package.

Improve Cash Flow

You can improve cash flow by increasing revenue—perhaps by increasing prices, changing product bundles and related pricing, focus marketing on proven ways to drive revenue, incentivizing and upgrading skills of salespeople to improve their performance, removing low-performers organization-wide, and sponsoring sales promotions. Ask suppliers for more favorable terms. Take advantage of cash discounts. Wherever possible, accelerate your collections. Renegotiating leases can improve cash flow, especially with assistance of a commission-based consultant.

Ignite Sales and Revenues

It's a red flag if your business is dependent on you as its main salesman. Revving up your sales staff is important when moving your business toward sale. One way to increase the revenue your sales staff generates is to seek sales channels outside your business. Strategic alliances can diversify sources of revenue and also can be a trial run of compatibility and value with a potential buyer. It can take at least a year to get an effective alliance program up and running.

Before selling your business may be the time to introduce new products, expand distribution channels, and enlarge your geographic presence. Depending on your time frame for selling, acquiring new business lines and entering new markets may also attract particular categories of buyers. Doing so requires more lead time and investment, however, so weigh return on investment carefully. Efforts such as these can take anywhere between one and three years to bear fruit.

Diversify Your Customer and Supplier Base

Another smart step to prepare your business for sale is to review and diversify your customer base, especially if you're dependent on a few customers. Further, seek customers who offer noncyclical demand to counter overdependence on cyclical or seasonal customers. A strong, diverse customer base radiates value and resilience that will pay off in the selling price of your business.

Being dependent on too few suppliers is also a weakness that may detract from your selling price. Accordingly, rectify deficiencies in your supply chain and inspect it for enhancement opportunities. Expand the number of your suppliers, especially those you rely on for critical inputs.

Diversifying your customer and supplier base can take between one and three years, so plan accordingly. That is not to say immediate changes can't happen or won't have impact. But we all know it takes effort to find quality partners at either end of the chain, and you shouldn't underestimate the effort.

Reduce Expenses

When preparing your business for sale, examine every expense to root out waste. Trim inessential expenses like entertainment and travel. Review utility and telephone costs, preferably by hiring a commission-based auditor. It may be worth appealing property taxes, renegotiating insurance coverage, and appealing workers' compensation ratings. Perhaps, it would be wise to convert leased and financed assets to owned assets. You might restrict advertising budgets to those expenditures that demonstrably improve sales. A concentrated effort could take three months. If you haven't been using a budgeting process, now is the time to start, for buyers could be interested in seeing your budgets.

Keep Your Operational Focus

Before putting your company on the selling block, do everything possible to maintain or grow revenue, profits, and margins—and maintain your operational focus on the business during sale negotiations. It's easy to take your eye off the profitability ball after deciding to sell and while entertaining prospective buyers. But you must assure your business meets, or exceeds, forecasts, or its valuation and potential sale may be jeopardized.

Document Your Business

Selling a business requires you to reveal vast amounts of information that may not be at your fingertips. Since the buyer will ask, you must organize contracts, records, and insurance policies and make them easily available. These documents will be needed during the selling process, and having them ready for review will increase your credibility and authority as a competent manager running a valuable business.

Corporate Records

The corporate record book and annual reports, if you're selling your entire business and not merely some assets, should also be readily accessible. Your corporate record book contains your original incorporation papers, business name registration paperwork, bylaws, trademarks, shareholder list, minutes of directors' meetings, and other documents. Small companies are sometimes lax here. If these don't exist or sorely need updating, your corporate attorney needs to get involved.

Documentation requirements may be less extensive for a limited liability company than for a corporation, but at a minimum you should expect to provide the company's formation documents and operating agreement if your company has one. Larger, multimember, limited liability companies often don't document minutes of membership meetings or written consents of members for actions taken, but they should be on hand.

Processes and Methods

Documenting key processes and methodologies will assure that important knowledge does not depart with anyone leaving your business, including you. Almost every organization has vital information that isn't written down. It is imperative to capture as much as possible to demonstrate viability and value to potential buyers and to assure a successful transition. This is particularly true for you as well as for workers and management who may leave or are nearing retirement. Operations and procedures manuals should be up to date. Some of these documented processes belong in the contingency plan discussed in a later chapter.

These are difficult efforts to estimate since they are dependent on the size of your business, state of your current documentation, and the complexity of your operations and methodologies. It can be useful to bring in consultants to work with your organization to produce high-quality manuals and other documentation.

Testimonials and Branding

To show off your business and its reputation, record and display customer testimonials and public relations activities that demonstrate your company's standing and prominence. Sale and marketing literature should contain current information, reflect your company's brand, and present it in a contemporary and consistent manner. This could be a three-month project if you dedicate resources to it. Brands do matter when it comes to selling a business and a strong brand in the marketplace is added value when it comes to selling.

Improving branding and name recognition, however, will be more time-consuming. Having a strong brand will very likely pay off, but it does require a longer-term investment.

Document the Human Element

As enterprises have flattened and deconstructed their hierarchies, jobs and paths within companies may have become obscure. In some businesses, particularly smaller ones, much of this never was formalized. Documenting the human element now, however, becomes important when you prepare to sell. Potential buyers will ask for human resources materials when appraising your business and its people as assets in a purchase. This is another project for which it is hard to affix a timeline. The length of time to complete depends on what you've done already and how recently.

Job Descriptions

Create job descriptions if none exist. They should be clear, detailed, relevant, and adaptable to a new owner. Employees' performance goals should be simple,

measurable, customer driven, and easily understood. Update performance eval-
uations and personnel files. Evaluate every position for outsourcing, automa-
tion, or elimination. Job levels might involve technical or managerial expertise
or a mix of both. It's important to define them consistently organization-wide
by level of responsibility and authority. Documented career paths should
show logical transition points to move up, down, and laterally within your
organization.

Organizational Structure

Review your organization structure and whether it effectively supports your
company's mission and goals. In smaller businesses, it may just be one boss that
everyone reports to. Are management structures and staffing as they should be,
especially considering an upcoming sale? Where does authority reside, and does
it address current needs and effectiveness? Are all of the dotted line relationships documented?

Several years ago we were consulting with a buyer during an acquisition, and
we noticed that the seller had promoted several people to grandiose titles right
before the sale. Suddenly, for example, there was a Chief Knowledge Officer
and a Chief "People" Officer. The seller's attempt to help his employees move
advantageously into the acquiring organization undermined his credibility once
it was discovered.

Undertake a structural review of job positions, work groups, and departments.
Decide which might be removed or added. For a smaller company, adding managers between you and the employees may make the business more transferrable
and therefore more valuable. What industry benchmarks are valid comparisons?
Could some employees be more effective in another position or with an investment in training? Which employees have a questionable future with the firm?
It's important that you deal with these issues before selling.

Compensation and Morale

Some buyers want to ascertain that employees are competitively compensated through salary, benefits, and incentives, whether they comply with rules
and regulations, and are well trained. All employee contracts need reviewing, including commission agreements, severance packages, and noncompete
arrangements, to see if they are in compliance, and to have them ready for the
buyer. Also, you need to document employees' terms, conditions, and entitle-
ment payouts.

There are many ways to take care of your employees. Consider offering critical
employees employment contracts, including "stay put" clauses for essential managers. You have to determine which employees are crucial to your business and
anticipate their reaction to your sale. Incentives such as bonuses or guaranteed

employment for a period after sale might encourage them to stay with the business.

Aside from key employees, are all employees generally satisfied? An employee turnover higher than the industry average can warn off potential buyers, so rectify its causes before your business appears on the market. We have seen the source of unrest surface in many different ways, from culture, to compensation, to safety issues. This can be a long-term effort to uncover and fix, and we recommend bringing in unbiased, trained experts to assist.

As a business owner, taking care of your employees and preventing layoffs may be a driving consideration for the sale. You should specifically target buyers that offer the least chance of that happening.

As painful as it is, in some instances layoffs will happen. Prior to entering into the sales process, you can put severance policies and packages in place. These may not survive the negotiation phase, but will set the bar to where you want it. In the letter of intent, you can describe how layoffs will be handled, provide severance pay and benefits continuation, and lay out whether you or the buyer are responsible for them. You can also negotiate assistance for displaced employees with a buyer. This could include help in finding new jobs by contacting state agencies or private firms to assist in outplacement.

Union Agreements

Potential buyers will ask when pertinent union contracts expire and whether negotiations are under way. You should examine contract requirements that might disrupt a sale and plan accordingly. Potential buyers will decide if changes are needed and whether that alters how they value your business. Understanding the situation does not itself take time, but dealing with what you uncover may. Be sure to consult competent labor counsel on these matters. Interpretation of labor contracts is complex.

Decision-Making

This is an excellent time to revisit the decision-making authority in your organization. Small firms tend to rely on the business owner only, and that may be a perceived weakness. Strong business leaders communicate decision-making guidelines and develop their management team's decision-making abilities. Decentralizing decision-making will strengthen your management team and your organization's post-sale viability. Demonstrating you've done so is crucial when preparing to sell your business.

Document Ownership of Tangible Assets

The philosopher Berkeley said, "To be is to be perceived." Sellers likely will pay more if they perceive your business to be an orderly, coherent, well-run enterprise.

Facilities

Improve your business's curb appeal. Spruced-up buildings, grounds, parking areas, signage, and equipment convey prosperity, productivity, and strong management. All should be in top-notch condition and show well. Display awards, affiliations, and citations prominently. Your physical plant and your offices should be organized and clean. These observable aspects speak as proxy for the thousand unseen things that are in the organization's DNA.

Online Presence

Just as you improve your physical business's curb appeal, so should you improve your online appeal. Ensure that you are using up-to-date, not necessarily state-of-the-art, web design and technology, that your online and off-line branding are the same and contemporary, and any posted materials—press releases, case studies, blogs, and the testimonies we recommend you update—are relevant, recent, and brand compliant. Conduct a web search on yourself and your company. Do you like what you see? Understand that potential buyers will go to your Web site and do an Internet search. You can put together a plan to project the image you want. This is an excellent opportunity for a smaller firm to create a professional appearance equal to or surpassing their larger company brethren.

Inventory

Often, owners keep inventory low prior to sale. Make sure your inventory is organized and presentable. Prepare records that verify cost and consistency of valuation. Items on consignment or sold but not shipped should be recorded as such.

Assets and Machinery

Draw up a detailed asset list and review the condition of machinery. Replace equipment that's obsolete or ending its useful life, or, if return on investment warrants, repair it. You may be tempted to reduce expenditures for repair and maintenance prior to sale. Savvy buyers, however, will realize that and reduce their offer price, knowing they must replace or refurbish equipment.

Customer Experience, Loyalty, and Service

Earlier we talked about both ends of the customer experience—first capturing diverse clients to broaden your customer base, and, once they have worked with your business, capturing current client testimonials. In preparing your business for sale, you should address the interim process of improving customer satisfaction and loyalty. If you don't already do so, invest in building a better understanding of your client base: geographic, demographic, behavioral, buying, and profitability characteristics. Using it to improve the customer experience, loyalty, and service can translate to higher and more profitable sales. This is an area where bringing in experts to build a plan of action and execute on it with your team could be very beneficial.

Technology

Assessing how your technology resources (software, hardware, and qualified staff) affect performance might show you how to enhance it. Update technologically deficient departments or invest in advanced production technology if return on investment warrants. Pay special attention to accounting or inventory management systems and upgrade them if necessary. A small firm can really shine here.

You can improve business processes and potential selling price by installing software that captures best practices. Choosing an industry standard over a solution that's technically stronger but less popular is recommended; the industry standard is more likely to be a potential acquirer's system, and thus easier to integrate when your firm is acquired. We have worked with companies that had a targeted buyer already in mind before they began the selling process. When it came time to upgrade their IT systems, they found out what sales software their ideal buyer had and installed it.

Installing a new enterprise-level system or targeted smaller application can enhance your selling price because it potentially enhances operations and enables management. It also contributes to the perception that your practices are up-to-date and your leadership is competent and forward thinking.

Document Intangible Assets

Many businesses large and small own valuable intellectual property (IP)—trade secrets, trademarks, copyrights, and patents that can be the most valuable asset of a business. You should register domain names, copyrights, trademarks, and patents. Unlike trademarks, patents have a limited life, so record when they expire.

A prospective buyer will insist on IP records, especially records documenting ownership. If your firm has significant IP assets, a formal intellectual property audit is essential. Your corporate attorney can direct you to experts who will appraise your IP and its transferability to a new owner. Also, you should determine the risk of potential infringement claims.

Settle Outstanding Actions

Resolve partnership and shareholder disputes and outstanding or threatened litigation as soon as possible. Document how you're mitigating risks of past or pending litigation. Pay outstanding judgments. Also, you should document how your business is complying with applicable regulations. Frequently, a prospective buyer will collect outside information on past and present lawsuits, your credit history and that of your business, complaints by consumers and public agencies, the official status of the corporation or partnership, and the existence of Uniform Commercial Code and tax liens. Be prepared to disclose and discuss issues that may surface.

Review Contracts, Leases, Licenses, Permissions

You may need a complete legal review of existing commitments before your business is ready to be sold. Be on the look out for change of control clauses in contracts. These may require you to either give notice to the other party that the ownership of the company is changing or obtain the consent of the other party to the transfer of ownership. In either case, if these clauses are not complied with the other party may have the right terminate the contract or pursue other legal remedies. A potential buyer will need to know what commitments you've made and how they affect doing business after sale.

Deeds

Many businesses own buildings included as part of the sale. You should be able to prove ownership through a deed, recent title search, or title insurance policy. Make available for prospective buyers all mortgages, deeds of trust, or other liens and debts that may affect title. If you prefer not to sell your company's real estate, consider situating it into a limited partnership or related legal structure. Doing so could generate an income stream for you if you lease to the new owner.

Environmental Audit

If your sale includes your company's real estate, understand that buyers increasingly insist on uncovering potential environmental problems before conducting due diligence. A Phase I environmental audit may be required to document the condition of the property. If problems are found, a Phase II environmental audit will conduct a detailed investigation of the issues and how to rectify them. Remedying the situation might improve your selling price significantly, but it also could lengthen the duration of sale or be prohibitively expensive. Not addressing the problem could make your business unsalable. You might consider selling your business without environmentally challenged assets.

Equipment Leases

Copies of leases for equipment and real estate should be reviewed and available. A critical, although unusual, issue is whether a landlord's consent is required for a new owner to run the business on the same premises. Other types of leases include office equipment, cars, trucks, and manufacturing equipment. Examine each to see if consent is required to transfer them to a new business owner, and renegotiate if necessary.

Employee, Customer, and Supplier Contracts

Other contracts to review before offering your company for sale include those with suppliers, customers, and employees. Are formal contracts in place where appropriate? Relationships that operate on a handshake may be less valuable to a potential buyer. Will contracts be transferable to a new owner? You should assure that important contracts are current, stable, transferable, and valuable. Know when customer and supplier contracts expire and, if necessary, extend them before selling your business.

Transferring contracts can be more onerous in an asset sale. Many have clauses requiring another party's written permission to transfer the contract to the buyer. If the buyer will assume prepaid expenses such as rent and insurance, you should verify and record that contracts are transferrable. Assure that insurance coverage is current and taxes are paid.

Licenses

Some businesses require licenses other than county or city business licenses. Restaurants, for example, must observe sanitation laws, and businesses selling alcohol must have a license because their product is regulated. Environmental laws require gas stations and dry cleaners to be licensed. Make certain that licenses and franchise contracts are transferrable and determine if they require renegotiation. Have these licenses documented and contact each issuing office to ask what, if anything, must be done when your business is sold. This is best accomplished early in preparing your business for sale. If there's difficulty or a delay in transferring ownership, it's best to know sooner so the sale won't be postponed.

Explore Other Ideas

Your plan for improving your business for sale is a matter of discovering what you can do and deciding what's most effective. Actions already discussed should be part of that plan. But there are several additional ways to spot improvements to include in your presale thinking.

Asking Questions

Ask yourself and those around you:

- What are our biggest challenges, and why are we facing them? Are our primary problems in our strategy, structure, technical capabilities, and culture? What are we doing about them?
- Where are gaps in our strengths and capabilities? What are our most promising unexploited opportunities or leveragable high-quality resources, and how can we realize their potential?

- What are our formidable barriers to needed changes? Are they technical? Cultural? Political?
- What initiatives are currently under way? Do they align and integrate with our goal of selling the business, and with sale-related activities?
- Are all necessary functions in place? Are some unnecessary or better outsourced?
- If we were to make a major investment, where would it be and why?
- What can we do to serve clients better? Are we capturing new ideas and acting on them?
- What information do we need and not have?
- Why do we win or lose business?

Adopt from Competitors

You may unearth other ways to improve operations and increase selling price by studying your competitors. Go beyond your conventional definition of who your competitors are and consider nontraditional competitors that might be able to enter your business's arena. This analysis also may help you to determine which competitors could be potential buyers. An investment banker could help with this determination as your selling process begins.

Small Improvements

Don't assume that all presale improvements require large teams, sophisticated software, and long time horizons. High-yield ways to improve the appeal of your business needn't be grandiose and expensive. Post-It Notes® on your wall to document work flow might be sufficient to guide you through simple and small enhancements. We have worked with companies on portfolios of quick hit business process improvement projects, such as accelerating proposal turnaround time, decreasing order errors, and improving product development processes and times. Small improvements are as beneficial as large improvements if they're the right improvements.

Conclusion

Energy and resources you expend in preparing your business for sale have many payoffs. They will, of course, boost the price you receive and help you protect those employees that made your business valuable, but your early efforts also may reduce time to complete the sale and transfer ownership. Several actions in this chapter—such as recasting financials and making operational enhancements—are highly recommended for every seller. Others might be less essential for you, perhaps because they don't pertain to your business or because you've been conscientious about them all along.

A key part of what we recommend you focus on is improving not just the operations or profitability of your business, but also its transferability. Contracts, customers, employees, suppliers, and capabilities are all valuable parts of the business you should be able to transfer and demonstrate transferability of to a potential buyer.

When contemplating new efforts and expenses in readying your firm for sale, evaluate and prioritize them by the operating efficiencies they produce and the potentially higher selling price that might result. Think through the eyes of the buyer. What is the value and how can you enhance it? This is where the early business valuation comes in, and your hard work to improve it. What are the risks and how can you mitigate them? A buyer will see the risks both in terms of things you can change and those you cannot change. Those that you can change are usually worth the effort. These include operating your business more profitability, ensuring your financial statements and balance sheet are healthy and correct, customer base is diverse, and management is capable and stable. Those items you can't change, such as business cycles, industry health, and interest rates, you can perhaps time if you have the time to do so.

Whether your sale is a sprint or a marathon, this kind of presale thinking will help you understand and focus on what's valuable and attractive to buyers while reducing their fears. You'll be confident you're offering them a higher-value firm. In turn, that confidence rightfully amplifies the sense of pride and accomplishment you've earned for years of hard work.

Takeaway Lessons

- Making your company ready for sale may be the most important thing you can do to attract an eager buyer and a top selling price. Thus, that same preparation also results in securing you greater means for the post-sale life you've planned.
- Your preparatory actions may be small and accomplished quickly or may be larger and more time-consuming, but you need to examine your operation from the boardroom to the mailroom to see what enhancements would improve your operations and valuation.
- Financially, it's usually necessary to recast historical financials to give a more accurate picture of your firm's potential. Be sure to obtain three years of audited financials as these will be requested by virtually any buyer. Operationally, you need to examine every moving part from your cash flow to your customer-supplier chain. Managerially, your scope of attention will range from reevaluating your organization's decision-making authority to updating its employee handbook.
- Designing and implementing these changes are also part of changing your involvement with your business. As you reshape your firm's future, you also shape your own.

For additional resources and tools, visit www.sellingyourbusinessformore.com

CHAPTER 5

What Is It Worth?
Valuing Your Business

Introduction

Putting a price tag on your life's work is no easy task. Though foremost in the minds of many business owners looking to price their businesses, valuation is more art than science. All business owners believe they have a good notion of what their business is worth and frequently have already designed their post-sale life based on that number. Their estimate may be based on a recent sale of a company in their industry or knowledge of their industry generally. It may, however, be inconsistent with how others view the business or not reflect how the market environment has changed. At the outset of your selling process, you should hire objective experts to assess your business's value. Set your expectations in the realistic range of prices they help to determine. Although experts will give you a thoughtful, thorough, and disciplined view of value, the market is always the final arbiter.

Valuing a business for sale is not simply a matter of math, and you need to understand the principles used. That knowledge will prepare you for the task you're undertaking. This chapter will focus on the three most critical and useful expressions of valuing a business: fair market value, strategic value, and multiples of earnings before interest, taxes, depreciation, and amortization. It will discuss each of these ways to assess value and explore when and why each is used. Further, it will explain how understanding the valuation generated by each approach gives you the underpinnings for restructuring ownership, preparing for the sale, and marketing your business. The chapter will not address the myriad other ways that businesses might casually be valued or those that have been in vogue at points in the past.

Three Measures of Value

When you hire professional appraisers and move toward sale negotiations, you'll encounter three commonly used measures of value for your business: fair market value, strategic value, and the multiples-of-earnings approach. One is likely to be preferable over another for your particular situation, although exceptions and combinations—for instance, selling selected assets separately—may prevail. Also, tax and gift considerations govern the valuation measure that pertains in your transaction.

Fair Market Value

Fair Market Value (FMV) is defined as the price at which a property would be exchanged between a seller who is under no compulsion to sell and a buyer who is under no compulsion to buy. It's assumed both parties have reasonable knowledge of all relevant information.

It's critical to understand FMV. It is the standard that federal tax law dictates for determining federal tax obligations arising out of gifts or estates. It has unavoidable implications for transactions or transfers that restructure ownership of stock among family members or family entities—for example, gifts of stock to children or to trusts for their benefit and sale of stock to related parties.

FMV is also an appropriate valuation to use in planning because it's an objective, supportable estimate. You can obtain a thorough professional valuation report by engaging an expert certified by the American Society of Appraisers, the American Institute of Certified Public Accountants, or the National Association of Certified Valuation Analysts. The narrow range of value identified in the resulting report will give you a sense of what price to expect in a transaction with a financial buyer, and it should serve as your minimum acceptable price in negotiating a transaction.

Fundamentally, FMV is the value at which a deal is an even trade—any reasonable buyer and seller would agree the price is fair and therefore would complete the transaction. There is a formidable quantity of history, case law, and IRS ruling pertaining to the standard of FMV. Although subtleties continue to be debated, the important aspects of this calculation of value are generally accepted.

Any business or interest in a business can be appraised under one of the following assumptions or premises:

- Your business is a going concern and will remain viable in the foreseeable future.
- The business's value is essentially an aggregation of the current value of its assets.
- The business is valued based on an assumption it will be liquidated.

Throughout this chapter, we assume your business is a going concern, an aggregation of assets, or combination of both.

In appraising your business as a going concern, a valuator will perform a financial analysis that employs three separate approaches to valuation. The *income approach* uses expected future cash flows of your business. The *market approach* is based on financial statistics reported by comparable public companies and on data for similar transactions involving public companies. The *asset approach* examines the value of your firm's underlying assets. Along with circumstances specific to your situation, weighted and consolidated information from these three valuation approaches will help to set your selling price.

An experienced business appraiser, however, employs a highly technical methodology. That methodology will include selecting an appropriate interest rate for calculating your cash flow, and it will calculate the effect of adjustments on your financial statements to "normalize" projections. The appraiser will examine your business's revenue and earnings trends and will consider similarities and differences in selecting public companies for comparison. To give you a finely tuned valuation, an expert appraiser will consider factors prevailing in the current market, your industry, and elsewhere.

Appraisers using an *aggregation of assets premise* will assess and assign a market value to each of your firm's assets and sum their values. If your company has two or more operating businesses, the process may require striking a value for each operating entity (which may involve a cash flow analysis and/or market comparable analysis). If your firm holds real estate or other hard assets to be included in your sale, the appraisal also would estimate their value. Cash or investments are added to FMV, and liabilities are subtracted.

Special considerations pertain if your company is a Subchapter S corporation. Its valuation will be affected by its pass-through tax structure, by its tenure in the holding period if it had been a Subchapter C corporation, and by built-in gains it might have.

Enterprise Value
Enterprise value is a key term in FMV appraisals and refers to the estimated overall worth of a business. Enterprise value is the sum of tangible assets, intangible assets (customer relationships, patents, trade names), and net working capital. Enterprise value minus the value of any interest-bearing debt is the value of your company's equity. A calculation of enterprise value is often the starting point for the calculation of the value of a block of shares in a corporation or a percentage interest in a partnership or limited liability company.

Levels of Value
Two important concepts in an FMV appraisal are *levels of value* and how an appropriately selected level influences the appraised value of the block or shares or interests in your business. Most commonly, these levels refer to the degree of control and marketability shareholders have over the interest being valued, but they also may be based on other attributes of your company and the market.

Control Premiums and Discounts
If you own the majority (or all) of your company's stock and can sell it without restriction, you own a *marketable controlling interest*. Your interest is marketable

because it can be offered for sale at your sole discretion, there is an active market in which to sell quickly, you are empowered to negotiate price and terms with a buyer, and you can execute the transaction. Your interest is controlling because you may hire and fire employees, set compensation, determine strategic direction and reinvestment of capital, set dividend policy, set or change capital structure, and make decisions about mergers, acquisitions, sales, or liquidation.

Marketable shares that do not represent a controlling interest are less valuable per share in calculating FMV. If you own less than half of your firm's stock and that stock can be readily sold at a liquid market price, you own a *marketable minority* (or *noncontrolling*) interest. The best example of this situation is owning stock of a corporation traded on a major exchange like the New York Stock Exchange or NASDAQ. Any shareholder of IBM is able to buy or sell shares any time but has no meaningful control of the business or influence over decisions with respect to it. The price at which a share is traded is a marketable minority value.

Usually, privately held businesses don't have marketable minority interests because there is no readily available market for disposing of the firm's stock. So shareholders who own less than 50 percent of a private company's stock have a *nonmarketable minority* interest. That is, a shareholder holding less than 50 percent of the company can neither sell the stock easily, if at all, nor control decisions made about the business.

Logically, as illustrated below, these three categories of interests will carry different valuations (figure 5.1).

A marketable controlling interest deserves the highest assessed valuation because its owner can sell at any time and can make operating decisions. In the illustration above, the valuation per share of this interest is $100.

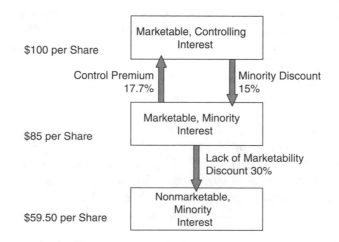

Figure 5.1   Levels of Value

Note: Please note that discounts in chart are for illustration only. Applicable discounts will be determined according to specific facts and circumstances.

An owner of a marketable minority interest in that same company may be able to exchange that interest for cash at any time. But because marketable minority interest confers only liquidity, not control of the company, its valuation will be less than that for marketable controlling interest. In our illustration, the value per share for a marketable minority interest is shown as $85, or $15 less than the $100 per share valuation for the marketable controlling interest.

Finally, the valuation of an interest that is both noncontrolling and nonmarketable—such as a minority interest in a privately held business—will be lesser still. In our example, valuation per share for a nonmarketable minority interest is $59.50.

The difference in share value for a marketable controlling interest and a marketable minority interest can be expressed in two ways. The $15 per share increase in valuation of the marketable controlling interest over the marketable minority interest is a *control premium*, typically expressed as a percentage of the marketable minority value. In this example, we would affix a 17.7 percent control premium. Looking at the same comparison from the higher valuation down, the $15 decline in value between marketable control and the marketable minority interest is a *lack of control* or *minority discount*. In this example, the lack of control discount would be 15 percent.

Comparing the nonmarketable noncontrolling interest to the marketable noncontrolling interest, the $25.50 difference per share captures the discount for lack of marketability. The discount for lack of marketability is 30 percent in our example.

Control premiums and discounts for lack of marketability and lack of control are grounded in real world fundamentals. As mentioned previously, the shareholder (or shareholders) owning more than 50 percent (or 66⅔ percent in some states) of the business controls the strategy, decisions, and determination to merge, acquire new entities, expand, or sell the business. Minority shareholders cannot in the usual course of business cause a company to be sold and cannot by themselves reorient its strategic direction. Therefore, there is considerable economic appeal in the power to direct the company and make decisions about its strategic direction. That economic appeal is reflected in the control premium. Lack of it is represented by the discount for lack of control.

Similarly, ready ability to liquidate an interest, liquidate the firm, or sell your business has inherent economic value. A reasonable buyer would pay more for property that could be sold easily than for property that's saleable only with difficulty or over an extended time. Marketability is more desirable than lack of it, and so it commands substantial incremental value as an asset.

Several factors influence assessed valuation of a minority interest in a closely held business. Valuation will generally include both a discount for lack of marketability and the discount for lack of control. The derived valuation, then, will be considerably less than a pro rata portion of the Enterprise Value of your whole company. In our example let's assume that there are 100 outstanding shares of ABC Company and that the enterprise value is 100 times $100 per share or

$10,000. A block of 20 shares, a nonmarketable minority interest, would be valued at 20 times 59.50 or $1190. On a pro rata basis, that same 20 percent of $10,000 would be $2000.

Volatility Discounts

During periods of volatility in the economy or markets, assessors may include volatility or arbitrage discounts in their valuation estimates. These discounts recognize the uncertainty of locating a buyer, the extended time involved to close a sale, and risk that a buyer might not close the deal due to unexpected financing contingencies or business uncertainty.

Value of Minority Interest

Assessed value of a minority interest in a closely held business will take in all applicable factors. The appraiser generally will base an assessment on enterprise value and then incorporate a discount for lack of marketability and a discount for lack of control. In weak and volatile markets, appraisers may carve out a further discount for volatility. Consequently, the final appraised value will always be less than the minority interest's pro rata value of the company as a whole.

Strategic Value

FMV defines the value of property exchanged between a reasonable buyer and seller with no compulsion to buy or sell. Routinely, however, a business is more desirable to some buyers than others. When a prospective buyer believes that acquiring a business or selected assets imparts a special advantage or will generate higher returns on investment, the transaction has *strategic value* to that buyer. A buyer who sees strategic value in the combined businesses would be willing to pay more for the business or assets.

For example, a buyer in the plastic extrusion business domestically purchases a European business with a strong distribution channel. The buyer can realize economies of scale by increasing its sales volume and may be able to move more product through developed distribution channels with little added cost. The European business has a higher strategic value to the U.S. buyer.

Since strategic value will be higher than FMV, it is in your interest to locate buyers who will pay a *strategic value premium*—that is, a higher sale price—for your business or its assets.

Multiples of EBITDA

This measure of value is often used in mergers and acquisitions. When a private or public company is sold, the transaction is often expressed in a *Multiple of Earnings Before Interest, Taxes, Depreciation, and Amortization* (EBITDA). An accounting number derived from a firm's income statement, EBITDA is a measure of free cash flow generated by a firm. It measures pretax cash flow before

Figure 5.2   ABC Company

maintenance, capital expenditures on facilities and equipment, and debt service. The dollar value of a transaction price may be stated as a multiple of EBITDA. In the example below, ABC Company had EBITDA in Year 1 of $10 million and a forecast EBITDA for Year 2 of $12 million. In January of Year 2, the company was sold for $60 million or 6 times (6x) *trailing* EBITDA (Year 1 result) (see figure 5.2).

Sometimes *forward-looking* EBITDA is the better measure. In this example, then, the $60 million selling price would be 5x forward EBITDA. Multiples of EBITDA available may vary dramatically across business cycles, from industry sector to sector, and for reasons specific to a company. The available multiple in a particular transaction may vary based on the company's history, forecasted future prospects, the size of the interest, whether the interest sold is controlling or not, the motivation of both parties, and other factors.

Middle market transactions, defined as those less than $500,000 in price, captured unusually attractive 8 to 10 and even 12 times multiples of EBITDA during the strong Merger and Acquisition (M & A) market of 2006 and the first two quarters of 2007. The ensuing credit crisis of later 2007 and recession of 2008 brought multiples in the 5 to 7 times range in a very stagnant transaction environment. Long term "normal" ranges for the broad middle market can be anywhere from 6 to 8 or 9 on average, but each industry's range is somewhat variable, and generally multiples are lower for very small companies and higher for those nearing $500,000.

Other Measures of Value

The most critical and useful measures of value to a seller are FMV, strategic value, and multiples of EBITDA. While we do not recommend using book value or rules of thumb in *any* assessment of value, they are so frequently mentioned that a brief review of each is worthwhile.

Book Value

Book value reflects historical value instead of current market value. It is an accounting term and not directly comparable to an FMV appraisal of a company or of an interest in a company. It does not purport to represent what a company or interest would command in an actual transaction. Book value is further dissimilar to market value because standard accounting practice requires valuing some assets at historical cost, not current market value.

In contrast, a market value calculation attempts to assess how the market prices your firm's assets or an interest in them at a current date. Also, value of intangible assets on a firm's balance sheet will influence book value but not market value. Book value often understates a firm's value compared to market value. In certain circumstances—for example, when assets are declining in price—book value may overstate a firm's worth to a buyer. Because of these inconsistencies with market-based value, book value is a poor basis for planning transactions or estimating sale price.

Rules of Thumb

In many industries, advisors and brokers have developed "rules of thumb" as a shorthand to valuing firms. Rules of thumb for a particular type of business may vary from one region of the country to another. Rule of thumb valuations are based on only one or two aspects of the firm's financial history and are therefore unreliable. A rule of thumb valuation usually will have little if any relation to actual market value of a firm, and if it does turn out to be a close estimate, it is largely by chance.

Industry rules of thumb may give you a notion of what your business is worth, but it's not a customized, reality-based number. Businesses are varied and complex, and their valuation needs to take that into account. However, since rule of thumb valuations persist in many industries, you should have an idea how they might apply to your business. In the best case, if the rule of thumb generates a higher potential sale price than a full valuation of your business, and the buyer is a relatively unsophisticated strategic buyer who relies on a rule of thumb, you may have leverage in negotiating price.

Uses of Different Standards of Value

Different valuation methods fit different situations. FMV is always the standard for gifts of property and is the standard for federal and local gift and estate tax calculations. It is also the standard of arm's length value in an Employee Stock Ownership Plan transaction or an installment sale between related parties. FMV must be used as the basis for valuing assets in a unit trust to determine the annual distribution amount, in assessing the initial value of property contributed to a Grantor Retained Annuity Trust, and in other applications where federal estate and gift tax implications arise.

Strategic value or synergistic value is an optimal value, for it includes the premium over FMV that a buyer will pay to acquire an asset imparting significant advantages.

When planning for a sale and considering possible selling prices, you should regard FMV as a floor and strategic value as the high end of possible price outcomes.

Valuation Is Critical

Most business owners start their selling process with a price in mind. It may or may not be grounded in reality. When considering selling part of your business or selling material assets, you should seek a professional valuation from an accredited business appraiser as a starting point. A formal valuation at its most basic will provide an objective range of values that you can use in wealth transfer planning and restructuring ownership as appropriate. If crafted well, a valuation will provide information about selling prices for similar businesses in the current market cycle, what prices have been historically, and how prices vary during upturns and downturns in the market cycle. A good appraisal also can provide insight into relevant value drivers of a given industry and what buyers in the market currently are seeking. Such insights can help you in preparing your businesses for sale and in marketing it to buyers.

Conclusion

Selling your business culminates years of effort, risks, and dreams. It means putting a price on your life's work, and it enables you to embark on new ventures professionally and personally. Despite the importance of valuation, it is still an art to arrive at a realistic number or range of value. In the end, the market at that moment and the buyers involved will determine the actual sale price of your business.

Takeaway Lessons

- Most owners have an end price in mind when offering their businesses for sale, but the fact is that valuing a business is an intricate and wide-ranging undertaking that merits hiring a professional valuation expert. It is exceedingly unwise to rely on book value, rules of thumb, or the most recent selling price of a similar business as a reliable gauge of your firm's selling price.
- The three most common professional measures of valuation are fair market value, strategic value, and multiples of EBITDA. Your wealth planning transfers will be measured at fair market value. You will get the highest price for your business if you find a strategic buyer willing to pay strategic value, which includes a premium for the efficiencies or synergies that buying your firm brings. You need to understand multiples of EBITDA because that is how prices are referenced when you are soliciting and executing a transaction. Both a fair market value and a strategic value can be expressed as a multiple of EBITDA.

- It's important to understand the principles of business valuation because they apply to other aspects of your transaction and have consequences for you and your family—including determination of income taxes, inheritance taxes, and allowable donations for gifts.
- Regardless of what you feel your business is worth or what an expert valuator estimates, there is only one absolute rule about establishing the selling price of your business: the market is always the final judge.

For additional resources and tools, visit www.sellingyourbusinessformore.com

CHAPTER 6

Setting the Stage:
Getting It Together Now to Enjoy Later

Introduction

Selling your business can generate sizable wealth for you and your family. But if you don't take proper precautions *before* selling your business, you'll pay a whopping percentage of that wealth in taxes—income taxes at the time of sale, gift taxes if you donate substantial sums to your family, and inheritance taxes that fall upon your heirs. You need a thoughtful, well-constructed plan to transfer that wealth in a manner that mitigates, and perhaps avoids, onerous taxes.

Establishing trusts to benefit yourself, your family, or your charities should be part of your wealth-transfer plan. In general, that involves shifting part-ownership of your company to trusts that benefit people you love and causes you support. As part of your wealth-transfer plan, trusts do more than minimize taxation. They may also allow your family and your favorite charities to share in the growth and gains of your business after you sell. This chapter discusses several types of trusts that produce these happy consequences and the concepts underlying them.

However, it's absolutely essential to keep four points in mind.

- First, you must integrate wealth-transfer planning into your total estate plan in ways that meet your values, goals, and desires for passing wealth on to others.
- Second, you also must integrate your personal wealth-transfer strategies into your business planning. Although trusts can produce extraordinary benefits, understand one thing especially: you're funding a trust with part-ownership of your business. You are, in essence, giving away part of your business—and, therefore, part of its income and future growth—to someone or something else. What's more, you're giving away a portion of the

control you have over your business. If you give stock in your company to a trust, the trust becomes entitled to all the prerogatives of an owner. Those include the right to review and object to your decisions, including your decision to sell your business. Seek advisors with detailed knowledge of your business-related documents and contracts, including buy-sell agreements, shareholder agreements, stock restriction documents, voting trust arrangements, or other controlling instruments.

- Third, you must create, design, and execute any strategy for estate planning, transfer of ownership, or tax planning only after rigorous advice from your accountant, trust and estate attorney, corporate attorney, and corporate trustee. Tax laws change maddeningly. Your strategies must change and evolve accordingly, and your plan must always accommodate your situation—which may also change as your life and goals go forward.
- Fourth, for your wealth-transfer plans to produce optimal results, you must complete them *before* selling your business—perhaps long before; in some cases, even before you ever disclose to anyone that you're *considering* selling.

In short, a sound wealth-transfer plan allows you to keep more of the money you receive from your life's work in building a business. But wealth-transfer plans should be tailored to your business, family considerations, extent of your wealth, what portion is represented by the value of your business, your desires and preferences, those of key stakeholders, and the terms of any applicable irrevocable trusts in your current estate plan. The rewards can be extraordinary, but so are the thought, preparation, execution, and understanding needed to yield those rewards.

Applicable Taxes

Before discussing wealth-transfer strategies, let's discuss the kinds of taxes that you can incur by selling your business and by engaging in strategies you take to minimize them.

Income Taxes

We needn't spend long on this subject. You doubtless have been paying yourself some salary as a business owner and perhaps have received interest and dividends from your company's portfolio or your own. You obviously paid taxes on that income. Our point is that under certain circumstances you also may pay income taxes on income generated within a trust or on loan interest payments you receive from trusts or other wealth-transfer vehicles.

When you sell something—including your business—you pay taxes on the difference between what you paid for it (*cost basis*) and the selling price you received when you sold it. That income is a short-term or long-term capital gain and taxed—under present law, anyway—at short-term or long-term rates. For purposes of this discussion, the important points are that you probably have a *zero cost basis* in the stock of your company, you likely have owned your company for an extended time, and therefore the entire amount you receive from selling your business will represent a long-term capital gain.

The trust to which you sell or donate your company's stock also will be vulnerable to income and capital gains taxes. Who pays them—you, the trust, or its beneficiaries—depends on the type of trust you create. The trust also has a cost basis determined at the time you sold or donated stock, and taxes apply to the difference represented by the eventual selling price. But again depending on the type of trust you create, you can maximize gains and minimize, perhaps eliminate, state and local taxes for whomever pays them.

Transfer Taxes

A transfer tax is one imposed on any exchange of property that reassigns ownership from one person or entity to another. We will focus on three kinds of transfer taxes: gift tax, estate tax, and generation-skipping tax. One or more of these may be imposed on any property—including your company's stock—that you transfer to someone else. Fortunately, however, besides levying transfer taxes the current tax law also allows several types of exemptions and exclusions.

Gift Tax

What constitutes a gift is a complicated and intricate question, which, again, is why you must have competent tax and accounting advisors. For our purposes, let's simply say that any time you give money or property—including giving your company stock to a trust—you potentially expose yourself to paying gift tax. When gift tax applies, you pay it, not the person or entity receiving the gift. Fortunately, tax law provides generous exclusions and exemptions.

You may make unlimited gifts to a spouse, who is a U.S. citizen, or to a qualified charity any time during life or upon death without incurring gift tax.

At present, you may give up to $13,000 yearly to as many recipients as you please without gift tax liability. The limit on this *annual exclusion* changes each year. Yearly gifts exceeding the exclusion incur federal gift tax. You must file a gift tax return and pay the taxes at the time you file your income tax return for the year you make the gift.

Besides the annual exclusion, tax law permits a *lifetime gift tax exemption*. While alive, you may make aggregate gifts up to a maximum exclusion limit without paying federal tax. In 2009 the exclusion is $1,000,000. Gifts exceeding your lifetime exclusion limit are subject to gift tax. They must be reported to the IRS and the gift tax paid in the year of the gift. Future federal tax legislation may further modify limits or change the rules completely.

Estate Tax

Estate taxes—also called *inheritance taxes* and, in some circles "death taxes"—are imposed by the state or federal government on property you leave your heirs when you die. All property you own, whatever the form of ownership, is potentially subject to federal estate tax.

Presently, you owe federal estate tax only if your property is worth at least $3.5 million when you die. But that is a sum well within possibility if you've been building your successful business for many years.

Any property you leave to a surviving spouse (if he or she is a U.S. citizen) is exempt from federal estate taxes.

Property you leave to a tax-exempt charity also is exempt.

The estate tax is scheduled to be repealed for one year in 2010, but as with all matters of taxation the door is constantly open to change. Be sure your advisors carefully monitor any tax law changes and modify your estate plan accordingly. Many states now also impose estate taxes.

Generation-Skipping Tax

The generation-skipping transfer tax applies to gifts you make while living or at death to grandchildren or individuals who are at least 37½ years younger. There is an exemption for this tax of $3.5 million in 2009. Gifts exceeding this amount made during life or at death are subject to gift or estate tax.

It can't be overemphasized how earnestly you need expert counsel when planning to minimize transfer taxes. Federal and state tax laws are subject to dramatic change over time. Federal gift and estate taxes are very substantial—currently, 45 percent. Therefore, you and your advisors would want to make full use of exemptions and exclusions, under the applicable tax code.

Let's examine customary tools and concepts that apply when you transfer shares or interests in your private business to family members or trusts. We'll then explore examples of how they might be used and the benefits they offer in the context of planning for eventual sale of your business.

Valuation

We introduced the concept of *fair market value* (FMV) in our earlier discussion of valuing your business for sale. You'll recall that *total enterprise value* is the gross measure of your company's worth. FMV is an estimate of what your company would sell for in a transaction between equally knowledgeable, willing, and unpressured buyers and sellers. We mentioned several concepts that go into determining FMV, including discounts for illiquidity, minority ownership, and market volatility. Just as FMV is used to set a value on your business prior to sale, tax authorities use FMV to assess value on the shares of your business that you donate to a trust. They use that value—along with adjustments of their own—to calculate potential gift taxes when you donate shares of your business to anther person or entity, such as a trust.

FMV and Transfers

In other words, an FMV appraisal of your company approximates what its stock would be worth if it were traded on a public exchange. Thus, FMV is the IRS standard for valuing transfers of property, including your company's stock, between related parties—for example, if you sell part of your business to your children or to trusts for their benefit. Under IRS rules, FMV is the standard for determining your transaction is arm's length, fair to both related parties, and doesn't represent a gift from parent to child or vice versa.

For instance, say you sold stock in your company to your children—or donated stock to trusts for their benefit—for less than the appraised FMV. The IRS could allege that the difference between FMV and your lower declared value represented a gift, not a transaction. As a gift, federal gift tax might apply. The same applies if your children paid more than FMV for the stock. The IRS might allege that the difference between the price paid and the lower FMV was a gift to you and therefore vulnerable to federal gift tax.

Fair Market Value versus Strategic Value

Ideally, you prefer to sell your business to a strategic buyer willing to pay a *strategic premium* above FMV because of synergies resulting when your companies are combined. However, even though your gift to a trust is appraised at FMV, the proper wealth-transfer vehicle enables you, your family, and your favored charities to later receive the buyer's strategic premium (see figure 6.1).

Note figure 6.1. The higher bar, strategic value, is greater than the financial value, which is calculated as FMV. The difference is a strategic premium. The difference between strategic value and financial value can increase the future worth of your company's stock held in a trust, because FMV incorporates a number of discounts.

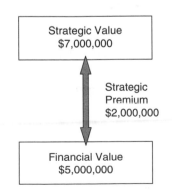

Figure 6.1 Strategic Premium

You should note, however, that while historically strategic buyers in almost every market are willing to pay the highest price for a desired target company, for the period from early 2006 through the third quarter of 2007 *financial buyers*—specifically, private equity firms—were paying higher prices than industry strategic buyers for attractive target companies. This anomaly occurred because private equity firms were flush with cash and reaching the end of their contractual investment period in their partnership agreements with investors. The firm managers needed to deploy the remaining funds within a short time or they would be compelled to return the un-invested capital to their investors. At the same time, credit was widely available and private equity firms could readily acquire substantial debt to fill out the capital structure in an acquisition to meet higher and higher prices. Although this effect was highly unusual, it is impossible to say it couldn't happen again.

Recall that when valuing minority interests in private businesses, FMV may incorporate discounts from a pro rata portion of the full enterprise value. Courts have recognized discounts for lack of control on blocks of shares or interests that represent less than 50 percent of the whole, and the IRS consistently has accepted valuation discounts for lack of marketability and lack of control on minority blocks of closely held stock. (H.R.436 has been introduced in the House of Representatives and if it passed into law, it would reduce or in some cases eliminate certain discounts for family enterprises.)

Other discounts also may apply. For example, during periods of volatility in the economy or markets, appraisers may factor volatility or arbitration discounts into valuations of private interests or stock.

Businesses in regulated industries may be eligible for additional adjustments or discounts, which accounts for the uncertainty of a buyer being able to timely acquire the necessary license. In the gaming industry in Las Vegas, for example, a casino's state-conferred gaming license is granted to the casino's owner or operator, not the casino. When a casino changes hands, the acquiring owner or his operator must request a new license to operate. Due diligence by the Gaming Commission is rigorous and time-consuming, and approval of the new license may take six to nine months, or in some cases never be granted at all.

Capturing Strategic Value

In other words, an FMV appraisal will include discounts for minority interests, market volatility, delays, and so on. Therefore, long before—two to three years, if possible—deciding to sell your company, you could transfer minority blocks of your business's stock to your heirs or trusts for their benefit.

If you make gifts directly to your heirs, those gifts will be subject to gift taxes unless they can be made within the restraints of the annual exclusion gifts, or your lifetime exemption. This may be practicable if your business is modest in value and you have many years lead time to make gifts. If you sell stock to children or grandchildren, be rigorous about the price and terms of the transaction as it will likely be subject to close scrutiny by the IRS.

When you give or sell these minority blocks of stock, your transfer is measured and taxed at FMV, including discounts. Later, when you sell your business to a strategic buyer, the sale price realized by the trust and its beneficiaries is the greater strategic value. They gain the premium between the strategic selling price and the discounted FMV assessed when you transferred the stock.

Further, by using techniques that transfer ownership long before you sell, you can diminish or avoid estate and gift taxes. Under some conditions and depending on the state where the owner and the business reside, some strategies also mitigate local and state income taxes on the gain if a sale occurs.

Values, Integration, Timing

Although there may be tax advantages to this planning, it's important to tailor your strategy primarily to carry out your wishes as to whom you would like to benefit from your wealth, future transaction or not. To be effective, transfer planning must serve your values and intent, as well as your cash flow requirements. Most strategies involve tradeoffs of control, tax mitigation, and complexity, and you should ask your advisors to explain these implications so you are confident you understand the advantages and disadvantages before making your decisions. You may be willing to forgo some potential economic benefit for the sake of a simpler execution. Or you may be comfortable with a complex or time-consuming strategy if it yields greater benefits. What's important is that your advisors integrate your strategy into your developed estate plan, that it furthers or at least does not impede your ability to sell your business, and that you are satisfied with the level of complexity and the result.

Ideally, two to three years before beginning to sell your business, you should review the ownership structure of your business and ask your trust and estate counsel and corporate counsel to explore alternatives and develop a plan. If you have only one to two years before selling, some advantages still will be available. With less than a year lead time, alternatives become more limited, but they're still worth discussing with your legal advisors.

Types, Uses, and Benefits of Trusts

Many wealth-transfer techniques involve transferring shares or interests to children or to trusts for their benefit. Such transfers are carried out by making a gift of those shares or interests, or selling them to the children or the trusts.

Important Definitions

A trust is a legal, fiduciary relationship in which an individual or institution, or both, holds legal title to property with the responsibility for keeping and managing it for the benefit of someone else (a *beneficiary*). A trust is created by a *creator* or *grantor* who executes a legal document that establishes the trust and outlines rules and guidelines for its management and disposition of assets. The grantor must fund the trust with property in order to make it effective.

Each trust is in effect for a specified duration, often many years, although some trusts have indefinite terms, Sometimes trusts will remain in effect for a specified period *or* until an event defined in its founding document occurs. At the trust's expiration, its assets are distributed to its designated *remainder* beneficiaries.

A *revocable trust* is one that the grantor can alter during his or her lifetime. An *irrevocable trust* cannot be amended or altered by the grantor. A *grantor trust* is structured so that the grantor pays the income tax on income and gains generated by the trust. In a *non-grantor* trust, the trust itself pays the applicable income tax.

The grantor will designate a *trustee* or *cotrustees* responsible for the trust's operation, paperwork, tax preparation if applicable, and disbursements to beneficiaries. If you fund a trust with your company's voting stock, the trustee will exercise shareholder voting rights.

Trusts commonly have two types of beneficiaries—an *income-taker* and a *remainderman*. The income-taker is entitled to current income generated by assets in the trust. The remainderman is the person or charity that receives the principal remaining in the trust when it terminates and its assets are distributed.

Grantor Retained Annuity Trust

A *grantor retained annuity trust* or "GRAT" is an irrevocable trust that provides an annual payment or *annuity* to the grantor during the life of the trust. Property is valued when it's contributed to the trust. If it is nonmarketable property—for example, stock of your privately held company—a professional appraiser calculates its value. The amount of the yearly annuity payment is calculated by multiplying that appraised value by a percentage specified in the trust agreement. For example, suppose the first year's valuation of the property year was $500,000 and the annuity percentage was 10 percent. Each year's payment to the grantor would be $50,000.

Under current law, the value of the gift to the trust is essentially the value of the property initially contributed minus the net present value of the annuity calculated based on a factor specified by the IRS. The stream of annual annuity payments paid to the grantor is not a gift subject to gift tax because it's returned to the grantor over time. GRAT's usually have two-year to five-year terms and are constructed so that the taxable gift is zeroed out and no gift tax is due (see figure 6.2). (Legislation has also been introduced in Congress which if passed into law would eliminate zeroed out GRATs.)

Figure 6.2 illustrates how the IRS formula works. This shows a four-year GRAT with an initial contribution of $1 million. We assume that the published

4 Year Term	Beginning Balance	2.80% Earnings	Annual Payout	End Balance
1	$1,000,000	$28,000	($267,742)	$760,258
2	760,258	21,288	(267,742)	513,804
3	513,804	14,387	(267,742)	260,449
4	260,449	7,293	(267,742)	0

Figure 6.2 Zeroed-Out GRAT

federal rate for the gift calculation on a four-year GRAT is 2.8 percent. In Year 1, the $1 million is placed in trust and earns a return of 2.8 percent or $28,000. The annuity payout to the grantor is $267,741.58. At the end of Year 1, there is a balance of $760,258.42, which will in turn earn another 2.8 percent or $21,287.24 in the second year. Again, the $267,741.58 annuity is paid. This calculation proceeds for the remaining two-year periods and, as you can see, there is no residual gift value at the end of Year 4. Because the formula zeroes out, there is no gift for federal tax purposes, and therefore no gift tax is due. However, if in fact this trust earned at a rate higher than the theoretical federal rate of 2.8 percent, there would be a residual value at the termination of the trust. That residual value would be distributed to the beneficiaries.

So a grantor can give business stock to a GRAT without paying gift tax if the GRAT is structured so that under the federal formula it will zero out. When the trust terminates, any residual stock remaining after the annuities are paid passes to the grantor's children or trusts for their benefit. A GRAT is successful if the property contributed appreciates at a greater rate than the IRS factor. To qualify for this tax-advantaged method of transferring property, the grantor must outlive the GRAT. If the grantor dies before the trust terminates, the trust is interrupted and its property reverts to the grantor's estate. If that occurs, the GRAT fails to accomplish the transfer of property to heirs.

Advantages of GRATS
GRATs have several benefits:

- If the property contributed is appreciating property, the beneficiary at the end of the GRAT term receives the property itself and the benefit of any appreciation in value.

- The property placed into the GRAT bears no gift tax and the residual value distributed is moved out of the estate of the business owner. No estate tax is due on that property at his or her death.
- The grantor receives an annual stream of income over the term of the GRAT.

Disadvantages of GRATS

- The grantor must survive the term of the GRAT, or all the property intended to be transferred to the beneficiary goes back into the grantor's estate.
- If the business declines in value or does not appreciate above the initial value, the GRAT fails.
- If closely held stock is to be part of the annuity each year, a valuation must be conducted to determine the correct number of shares that fulfills the value of the annuity.
- The complexity of the GRAT deters many candidates.

Usually, property placed in the GRAT includes income-producing property, cash, or marketable securities so that liquid funds are available each year for the annuity payment. If there's insufficient cash, the GRAT may provide that illiquid property (for example, private company shares) may be paid to satisfy the annuity.

Example of a GRAT

Here's an example of using a GRAT to move value from a closely held business to the next generation. For simplicity, let's assume a gift of stock to the GRAT and disregard whether it appreciates in value while inside the trust.

Susan owns a warehousing company with an enterprise value of $10 million. She gives 40 percent of her stock to a GRAT for the benefit of her son Owen. The underlying pro rata value of 40 percent of the company is $4 million. However, Susan's gift is a nonmarketable minority interest, so its appraised FMV is $2.8 million. Assume Susan's GRAT has a four-year term and the required IRS factor is 2.8 percent. The annuity paid to Susan, which will zero out the value of the gift in the GRAT, is calculated at $749,700 for each of the four years. In this case, Susan's yearly annuity would be paid in stock, not cash. If Susan's company appreciates 10 percent a year, its enterprise value will be $14, 640,000 at the end of four years. Because of the appreciation of the company, when the GRAT terminates, there will still be stock left in the GRAT equal to 6 percent of the company. That stock will be distributed to Owen outright, and Susan paid no tax.

If Susan wished to transfer more to Owen, she could repeat the process with another GRAT. If Susan later sells her company to a financial buyer for $14,640,000, Owen receives $878,400 minus tax. If she sells to a strategic buyer who pays $16 million, Owen receives $960,000 minus tax.

If Susan had instead given 6 percent of her company to Owen that first year, she would have to have counted the gift against her annual exclusion and her lifetime exemption—or pay gift tax that first year if she had already exceeded the permitted exclusion and exemption.

Intentionally Defective Grantor Trust (IDGT)

This is a completed irrevocable trust designed so that the grantor—not the trust or its beneficiaries—pays all taxes on income the trust produces. An IDGT appeals to parents wishing to transfer assets from their estates to their children, but they want to avoid saddling the children or the trust with additional taxes. Sometimes an IDGT can be modified later so the income tax obligation reverts to the trust or beneficiaries. This modification may be desirable if a long-term trust is expected to accumulate ample cash to pay taxes or if children will reach adulthood able to pay tax on their share of trust income.

Installment Sale

When selling your business in an *installment sale*, you accept a promissory note from the buyer instead of cash. The note requires the buyer to pay you a specified amount over a specified period at a specified interest rate. Under this arrangement, you defer income taxes on the sale of your business. You pay ordinary tax rates on interest you receive from the note. But you pay a lesser capital gains tax for the portion of the capital gain received each year.

Sale to a Defective Grantor Trust

The following example illustrates your benefits from selling some shares of your business to a defective grantor trust for the benefit of your child.

Fred owns 100 percent of a chain of movie houses worth $50 million. He decides to sell a 35 percent block of shares to an intentionally defective grantor trust to benefit his daughter Lily. Fred names his brother Tom and the Southern Trust Company as cotrustees of the IDGT. The 35 percent block of shares has an underlying value of $17.5 million and is appraised at an FMV of $12,250,000, incorporating a 30 percent combined discount for lack of control and lack of marketability.

Fred makes a seed gift of cash to the trust of 10 percent of the value of the stock or $1,225,000 so that the trust has initial liquidity. Dividends from the stock paid to the trust will provide further ability to make installment loan payments to Fred. Fred then sells the stock to the trust at FMV and takes back a note from the trust. Terms of payment provide for the trust to pay Fred interest for three years and then pay principal and interest in installments over the remaining 12 years at an applicable federal rate (AFR) of 5 percent. The note is secured by the 35 percent block of movie house stock.

What did this accomplish? Fred was able to transfer $17.5 million in underlying asset value (35 percent pro rata value of the total $50 million enterprise value) to an irrevocable trust for the benefit of his daughter Lily for the price of $12,250,000. Since this qualifies as an arm's length sale (the price is set at FMV, the note is secured with stock, and promissory note interest is at the AFR interest rate), there is no gift tax on the stock now in the trust. Further, let's assume a gift tax rate of 45 percent on the $1,225,000 cash gift to the trust; Fred would have paid gift tax of $551, 250 in the year the IDGT was funded.

Because it's a grantor trust, Fred owes future income tax on dividends or capital gains from the trust's stock. However, interest payments he receives from the promissory note largely offset the owed taxes.

Benefits Received

If Fred sells his business three years later to a strategic buyer for $60 million, what happens? (see figure 6.3).

Assuming Fred's cost basis in the company was $0, and ignoring income taxes for simplicity, Fred nets $50,674,000 after deducting gift tax paid when the trust was funded. The IDGT benefitting Lily reaps $8,775,000—the realized value of the underlying stock minus the price it paid to buy the stock plus the strategic premium on 35 percent of $10 million. Total value to the family is $59,449,000.

	Before Sale to IDGT	After Sale to IDGT	Sale of Company Three Years Later at $60,000,000
Fred	Owns 100 percent of Company $50,000,000 in value	Owns 65 percent of company $32,500,000 in value	Receives $39,000,000 Less $551, 250 Plus $12,225,000 Net proceeds of $50,674,000
IDGT Trust	No Ownership	Owns 35 percent of Company $17,500,000 in value Owes $12, 225,000	Receives $21,000,000 Pays back $12,225,000 Net $8,775,000
Pros	Fred controls all stock.	Fred still controls company with 65 percent of stock gain recognized overtime-installment sale.	
Cons		IDGT owns and votes 35 percent of stock Fred pays gift tax of $551,150 on cash gift	

Figure 6.3 Sale to an IDGT

	Before Sale to IDGT	After Sale to IDGT	Three Years Later Sale at $78,000,000
Fred	Owns 100 percent of Company $50,000,000 in value	Owns 65 percent of Company $39,000,000 in value Pays gift tax of $551,150 on cash gift pays	Receives $50,700,000 Less $551,150 Plus $12,225,000 Nets $62,374,000
IDGT	No ownership	Owns 35% of Company $17,500,000 in value Owes $12,225,000	Receives $27,300,000 Pays back $12,225,000 Nets $15,075,000

Figure 6.4 Sale to an IDGT Plus Appreciation

What if, instead of using an installment sale, Fred had simply given 35 percent of his company's stock to a trust for Lilly three years before the sale? With a federal gift tax of 45 percent, he would have had to pay $5.5 million in gift tax. Fred's net sale proceeds after gift tax would have been $33.5 million. The IDGT for Lily would receive $21 million. Total net proceeds to the family would have been $54.5 million.

What if Fred's business appreciates 30 percent to $78 million over three years? (see figure 6.4).

In that scenario, Fred receives $50.7 million before income tax for his 65 percent share minus $551,150 in gift tax plus the payback from the IDGT of $12,225,000 for a sum of $62,374,000. The IDGT for Lily receives $27.3 million, pays Fred back $12,225,000, and nets $15,075,000 before income tax. The family in aggregate captures $77,449,000 pretax on the sale to the strategic buyer. If, instead, Fred merely gave the stock to the IDGT, he would have the same $5.5 million gift tax bill noted a moment ago. So he would net $45.2 million before income taxes, and the IDGT would net $27.3 million before income taxes. The family would receive only $72.5 million.

By engaging in the installment sale three years before selling, Fred has transferred over $15 million to a trust for Lily while paying almost no transfer tax. Also note that since Fred retained 65 percent of the stock, he continued to be the controlling owner of the business until the final sale.

Dynasty Trust

A *dynasty trust* is a trust that is permitted to have a very long (sometimes indeterminable) term. A dynasty trust is appropriate when you intend to keep your business flourishing through multiple future generations. Because the trust remains in effect at least as long as ninety-nine years, assets typically are invested to meet the financial needs of a growing number of beneficiaries in each generation.

You might put stock representing a minority interest of your business in a dynasty trust with the hope your business will prosper and benefit succeeding future generations. But if you sell your company, the portion of the *proceeds* realized on the stock of your business will not be distributed to the beneficiaries as in other trusts. Instead, they will be invested within the long-term dynasty trust. Your sale still benefits future descendants. If you sell, it likely will be to a buyer who will pay you a strategic premium, and the dynasty trust will reap that strategic premium. And as with a GRAT or a defective grantor trust, no gift or estate tax applies on appreciation of stock in a dynasty trust.

Many states presently permit dynasty trusts. Even if your state does not, you may be able to avail yourself of this option by creating a trust in a state that does. Each year more states are adopting laws to permit them.

Delaware Non-Grantor Trust

This trust is a specialized vehicle presently available only in Delaware. The name refers only to the fact that income tax obligations of the trust do not flow to the grantor, but remain in the trust. There *is* a grantor who creates the trust. Unlike most other trust instruments, its unusual feature is that the grantor or creator of the trust can be one of its beneficiaries. The trust must have a Delaware trustee and has somewhat complex rules for making distributions. It requires a distribution committee to evaluate and rule on any requested or proposed distributions. Theoretically, this is to keep deliberations evenhanded, and a distribution to any beneficiary, including the grantor, will be fiduciarily sound. If the required conditions are met, federal and state governments tax the trust as a separate entity for income tax purposes, and income is not taxable to the grantor. Moreover, the trust is considered a Delaware entity and, thus, the state where you live might not impose local taxes.

The example below demonstrates one way you might benefit from a Delaware non-grantor dynasty trust.

William is a New York City resident who owns $100 million of zero-basis stock in his privately held clothing retailer, Apparel, Inc. William creates a Delaware non-grantor dynasty trust. He places $50 million of his Apparel stock in the trust, hoping his descendants will benefit from his burgeoning business. Years later, William and his co-owners sell Apparel to a private equity firm for cash. Each $50 million block will be worth $75 million in cash at the closing. Assuming a 15 percent federal capital gains rate, New York State and City income tax rates of 10.49815 percent, and a Delaware state income tax rate of 0, the after-tax value of each block of stock is as follows (see figure 6.5).

The tax benefit of the Delaware strategy is $7,873,500 because Apparel stock in the Delaware trust escapes local and state income tax. The nearly $64 million will be invested within the Delaware dynasty trust and will continue to benefit William's descendants. Moreover, since the investments remain in the dynasty

	Delaware Trust stock	New York state personal stock
Sale value	$75,000,000	$75,000,000
Fed cap gain tax	11,250,000	11,250,000
NY state, local tax	0	7,873,500
Post tax value	**$63,750,000**	**$55,876,500**

Figure 6.5 Tax Benefit of a Delaware Trust

trust, estate taxes (but not generation skipping taxes) will be deferred on its capital for generations.

Charitable Lead Trust

This type of irrevocable trust makes an annual payment to a qualified charity for several years or until a previously stipulated event occurs. On either occasion, the trust terminates and its remaining assets go to the designated remainder beneficiaries, who are persons or organizations that aren't charities. In the year you create the trust, you may claim a charitable tax deduction for the amount of the income that goes to the charity. However, the remainderman is not a charitable organization. Therefore, only part of the value of the property you gave to the trust qualifies as a charitable gift. Of course, the value of the non-charitable remainder counts toward your lifetime exclusion or gift tax calculation.

Charitable Remainder Trust

As when creating a charitable lead trust, you fund a *charitable remainder trust* (CRT) by donating partial ownership of your company to a charity before you sell. However, the CRT pays you an annuity each year until death, at which time the CRT's assets belong to the charity. Applicable tax rules are the reverse of the charitable lead trust. As the grantor, you claim an immediate income tax deduction for the net present value of the remainder amount going to the charity. Income tax may apply to the stream of income to you.

Giving a minority share of your company to a charitable trust or other qualified charity may generate substantial value to the charity while offering you income tax and transfer tax benefits. However, you must give the charity your business stock before you have a definite intention to sell, or you forfeit the tax advantages. For complex strategies involving gifts of business interests or stock, consult experts—trust and estate attorneys, corporate attorneys, and professional appraisers. Rules are complicated—especially for Subchapter S corporations and partnerships and, like all tax law, are subject to change.

Conclusion

When you receive substantial wealth, with it comes the possibility of substantial tax burdens for you, your family, and your heirs. A strategic wealth-transfer strategy is essential if you are to minimize the tax consequences for everyone who deserves the maximum return for years of support while you grew and managed a prosperous business. However, that strategy must begin before you sell your business. It must merge with your overall plans for your estate and for your business. It must reflect your wishes and values. Above all, it must be created and implemented with guidance from competent and experienced tax, estate, and accounting advisors.

Takeaway Lessons

- Your business is more to you than money. But when you're paid for your life's work it's with money, and you'd like to keep more of it. One way to do that is by establishing one or more among several long-established types of trusts.
- Besides reducing the tax bite, you may provide in different ways for yourself, family, heirs, and charitable interests through a trust arrangement. You may arrange a combination of income and capital gains, time horizons for receiving payments, and distribution of proceeds upon specified times or events. But often there are rigorous and intractable rules and time specifications to be met, so legal and financial counsel is essential.
- As with so many issues in selling your business, the time to consider taxes and trusts is before your business goes on the selling block. But if you take the proper steps at the right times, a trust can convert the selling price of your business into a lifetime of lesser-taxed rewards.

For additional resources and tools, visit www.sellingyourbusinessformore.com

CHAPTER 7

Assembling Your Own A-Team

Introduction

Selling a company is, by necessity, a team effort. Most successful entrepreneurs spend a lifetime building a single business. They are experts in their industry and adept at growing revenues and earnings, refining product lines, and adapting business strategies to competition and changing markets. However, they have little hands-on experience selling a company. This is the time to call on experts who sell businesses as a profession. This chapter examines which advisors you already have and which you might need to add to your team. We'll discuss the role each advisor should play and suggest guidelines for selecting the best advisors to complement your objectives.

Present and Long-Standing Advisors

Preparing your business for sale, developing a strategy, marketing, negotiating the deal, and closing the transaction involve a number of specialized players besides you. The wise entrepreneur will assemble those essential team members early in the selling process. Let's first consider the advisors you already rely upon and what they contribute to the massive project of selling your business.

Corporate Attorney

For many years you've likely had a trusted corporate attorney, someone who knows you and your company and understands how it evolved, both internally and as a business. If your company has an internal general counsel, an outside counsel from another firm probably will have worked closely with him or her. If your firm has no general counsel, your external corporate counsel likely will have acted as your general counsel.

Your attorneys probably drafted your bylaws and articles of incorporation and were involved in creating and counseling your board of directors or advisory board. They will know details of buy/sell agreements, shareholder agreements, restrictions on transfers of stock, management contracts, pension-benefit plans, and related matters. If your business was created as a Subchapter S corporation or elected to convert to Subchapter S from Chapter C, your attorneys would know what implications that might have for selling your business. If your company has unionized employees, your corporate attorney or attorney at an outside firm will understand implications of existing union contracts on your sale.

Over and above legal matters, your attorney likely has been a reliable, knowledgeable confidant regarding strategic business decisions. Such broad knowledge of your business's evolution, its legal landscape, and the resulting constraints and possibilities will be helpful in developing a sale strategy and identifying elements critical to confidentiality agreements, the offering memorandum, the concluding contract, and related legal agreements.

During your selling process, your attorney may play many roles, such as aiding in restructuring your business, drafting board resolutions, drawing up management contracts, and creating other internal agreements. Most importantly, your attorney will remain a trusted sounding board on strategy for your business.

Accountants and Auditors

Your accountant knows the financials of your business and is your chief resource for tax questions. He or she prepares your financial statements and tax returns. If your company has not historically kept audited financial records, your accountant or external auditor from an accounting firm will prepare historical and current audited financial statements in preparation for the sale. Prospective buyers nearly always require these documents for an objective, authoritative view of your company's financial performance.

Chapter 4 mentioned recasting financial statements to "normalize" expenses, earnings, and taxes to reflect your company's operating potential. The accountant along with your CFO or controller and external auditor will be the experts who do the recasting.

During the course of developing a sale strategy and identifying appropriate buyers, your on-staff or external accountants can prepare an analysis of liquidity scenarios, showing the before-tax and after-tax results of alternative strategies—for example, a stock sale versus an asset sale. Such analysis will aid in identifying and prioritizing strategies for sale.

If you're considering a particular buyer and have access to that buyer's financials, a good accountant can construct theoretical pro forma financial statements of a combined company, which may give the buyer worthwhile insight into your company's potential value. Analysis of this type also helps you considerably in choosing a strategy to obtain the buyer's top-of-the-range offer.

Your accountant (with your CFO) will help to supply data included in an offering memorandum and to establish a physical or electronic data room where serious prospective buyers may perform due diligence on company records, financials, and contracts.

Key Managers: COO, CFO, General Counsel

Cooperation of senior company officers is paramount for a successful sale. For an optimum sale, your business must continue to run smoothly and, if possible, post growing earnings. The chief operating officer (COO), chief financial officer (CFO), general counsel (or outside attorney), and managers of key disciplines will be involved in presale "clean-up-and fix up" activities. These executives will have knowledgeable insights into your industry and competitors, and they will understand the strengths, weaknesses, risks, and opportunities within their domains. The presence of good, capable, professional managers indicates a disciplined company and makes your company more attractive to buyers, especially private equity buyers and strategic buyers who are expanding vertically or geographically. You should identify the managers to include in your selling strategy team and incentivize them to remain through the process and work for your objectives. If you have ample lead time of two to three years, you may be able to construct incentives that are either stock-based or tied to increases in stock value over that time. Consult with your accountant to determine if the payoff at sale for these key managers can be structured as a capital gain instead of ordinary income.

These managers will contribute to the narrative of the marketing memorandum involving their areas of responsibility. Potential buyers likely will interview them during due diligence to learn about operations under their jurisdiction and to evaluate them for continued service. If management presentations are part of marketing your business during sale, you will ask the best of your principal managers to present.

When you have a board of directors, you might include its chairman, selected directors, or a special committee of the board in your sale effort. Independent board members may be an objective resource for evaluating alternate liquidity options or for selecting the strongest buyer candidates. In addition, of course, the board and company shareholders will approve the final deal.

Family Members

Family members whom you choose to help with the sale should have strong interests in the company and be able to view a possible sale dispassionately. The best family members for this responsibility will be thoughtful and deliberative, have a business background or training, be objective about the sale, and be collaborative team players.

Financial Planner

Your financial planner will create a comprehensive financial plan that will out-line how you can improve your asset base and design cash flows to meet your financial objectives and goals. This consultant can be enormously helpful in working out in specific details what you will need financially to support your lifestyle and dreams for after the sale. Planners are licensed by the Securities and Exchange Commission, National Association of Securities Dealers, and some-times state insurance commissions. Many also have earned designations such as Certified Financial Planner (CFP) or Chartered Financial Analyst (CFA).

Insurance Professional

You probably have an insurance broker or advisor who has helped you with life insurance, key person insurance, or comprehensive policies covering risks inherent in your business. Keep this professional in the loop. If you have taken out split-dollar policies or other business-owned policies on yourself or your executives, you eventually may want to transfer these out of your business to other entities or individuals personally. As you modify your estate plan and reas-sess your potential wealth, you may wish to incorporate some insurance-based solutions to fund obligations such as future estate tax payments. Your insur-ance specialist can help you sort among cost-efficient and practical strategies to accomplish these ends.

Additional Advisors to Bring Aboard

Certainly, professionals whom you have traditionally relied on for counsel and help in running your business will be part of the team involved in selling it. But the difficult and demanding process of sale requires specialized counsel.

Valuation Professional

We've made repeated references to the importance of obtaining a valuation of your business when you begin planning your sale. Seek a professional specifi-cally qualified to perform business valuations. Be sure that the professional you select is certified by the American Institute of Certified Public Accountants, the National Association of Certified Valuation Analysts, or American Society of Appraisers (ASA). Do not confuse the ASA certification for *business appraisal* with the ASA certification for *real estate appraisal*. They are separate and distinct training programs.

Estate Planning Attorney

As we discussed in chapter 6, presale restructuring of your company's ownership through gifts of stock or assets can benefit your estate planning and mitigate taxes. Include your estate planning attorney in your team of advisors before you market your company for sale. It may take considerable time to choose the appropriate estate planning techniques and integrate them into your long-term objectives for yourself, your family, and your company.

Trustees

If a family trust or multiple trusts owns shares or interests in your company—or will own shares via a presale restructuring of your company's ownership—trustees must approve any transaction pertaining to sale or merger of your company or disposal of its material assets. Trusts that own your company's voting stock are fully empowered shareholders. Their trustees and cotrustees bear a fiduciary responsibility to evaluate terms of the sale and to satisfy their questions or concerns before voting on the transaction. Trustees must ascertain that the sale price is reasonable and represents at least fair market value, and that the transaction is fair to current income beneficiaries and future remainder beneficiaries. Therefore, capable and conscientious trustees can provide a valuable soundness check for your overall deal.

You should choose trustees carefully while you develop and hone your estate plan. Trustees will not only be intimately involved in your sale transaction but will be close family advisors for perhaps several generations. You can select an individual for this role, an institution, or a combination of both. In looking for an individual trustee, consider a family member, a close business associate, or your accountant or attorney. Choosing one of your business managers is usually a poor idea because that may create conflicts of interest for them with respect to a sale or restructuring of your business. For example, if a future buyer offers a good price and reasonable terms for your company but the deal anticipates that key managers will lose their jobs, a manager/trustee who wants to keep his job may vote against the deal. However, from the perspective of a trust for the benefit of grandchildren, the deal is lucrative and therefore favorable. If you do select an individual trustee, be sure to name a successor trustee and create a mechanism for series successor trustees to be identified.

If you name an institution as trustee (a *corporate trustee,*), you get the benefit of broad fiduciary experience, institutional history, knowledge of your family and its needs, and access to the many resources of a full service institution. Look for a bank with a strong fiduciary reputation and practice, and be sure it has deep capability and experience with family businesses in a trust environment.

We recommend a combination of cotrustees with both an individual and a corporate trustee. This arrangement gives you the best of both worlds. The individual trustee will know the family situation intimately, understand the values underlying the language of the family trusts, and will be personally aware of shifting needs and circumstances of various beneficiaries. The corporate trustee brings a wealth of wisdom about managing trust assets and can assist beneficiaries with discretionary distributions in a way consistent with the grantor's wishes as set forth in the trust agreement. Corporate trustees also can summon trained resources to analyze complex financial, tax, or legal quandaries arising from the trust. Most important, institutions don't get sick or die or become unable to manage the ever-complex affairs of a fiduciary relationship.

Involving trustees early avoids delays in finalizing the sale. If trustees are familiar with your transaction, able to comment on drafts of transaction-related documents, and informed as changes develop, they may be more inclined to support the sale. If trusts involved have corporate trustees or cotrustees, inviting them into the planning stages might be advantageous. Corporate trustees often have extensive transactions expertise and may offer thoughtful advice throughout the sale.

The Transaction Attorney

Selling a business is a specialized discipline within a law firm's corporate practice. In seeking the right transaction specialist, you should look for an attorney who's concluded many deals, preferably in your industry and within the size range of your particular deal. He or she should be a knowledgeable strategic thinker and experienced at negotiating terms and drafting purchase and sale agreements favorable to sellers.

Knowledge of industry norms and of general terms covering recent transactions can provide significant negotiating advantage for you as a seller. In some cases, it's desirable that the transaction attorney has completed deals in your locale through which he or she has gained an understanding of local norms, ordinances, or zoning. This may be essential if real estate is part of the sale or if an industry is tied a specific place—casinos in Las Vegas or film companies in southern California, for instance.

Investment Bankers

An investment banking firm offers you a portfolio of valuable services, and a capable and experienced one is essential to your sale for two reasons. First, it is in the market constantly. It can assemble information about the range of sale valuations in ongoing or former deals within your industry and translate that into a range of potential selling values for you. Second, an investment banking firm has a network of resources and data to identify potential buyers beyond the usual suspects of close competitors and major public companies in your industry. A good investment banker can contact potential buyers domestically and internationally, discover buyers seeking to integrate or acquire, and approach private equity funds that may be open to investment in your business. There are many good investment banks focused on middle-market businesses with values from $20 million to $500 million. A handful of boutique banks target even smaller businesses—from $5 to $20 million—but still offer full professional banking services.

The investment banker will draft and assemble your principle marketing materials, including teaser communication and the information memorandum. With input from your business and other team members, investment bankers will propose the appropriate positioning of you in these documents and in contacts with buyer candidates. It will initiate contact with the best potential buyers and present tailored selling pitches to them.

The investment banker will advise your team and suggest a marketing approach appropriate for the business and economic situation—for example, whether to auction your company broadly or to pinpoint a few potential buyers. When initial expressions of interest emerge and the most promising are identified, an investment banker will analyze candidates to assure that only financially sound prospects are approached for negotiations. Investment bankers will try to create competition among interested and financially sound potential buyers so negotiations start at a higher opening price. With you and your other advisors involved in deliberations, investment bankers will evaluate, compare, and contrast serious offers. If you wish, the investment banker may be your lead negotiator for price and terms.

Choosing External Advisors

If you need to find an estate planner, start by asking for recommendations from your existing advisory team, particularly your outside CPA firm, corporate counsel, financial planner, or business banker. You can get suggestions from professional organizations. The American College of Trust and Estate Counsel (ACTEC) has lists organized by state of member professionals on its Web site www.actec.org. Or you can check with your local or state bar associations for qualified estate planners in your area.

You should look for a transaction attorney and investment banker with experience in your industry and experience negotiating deals of a size comparable to your transaction. Along with their sterling professional credentials, advisors should be personally compatible with you and your selling team. The selling process may extend over months and be complicated and stressful. There is no place for prima donnas. You need advisors with the credentials and temperament to work collegially.

Equivalent Expertise

It is essential that your advisors equal the sophistication, expertise, and experience of a buyer's advisors. For example, prospective buyers from private equity firms or Fortune 500 companies likely will be advised by prestigious law firms and reputable investment bankers. Your advisors should be comparable in quality and experience to assure your strategy and negotiations are on equal footing. As the process moves to drafting purchase and sales agreements—especially representations, warranties, and escrows—expert legal counsel will assure that you are not disadvantaged.

We have seen more than one middle-market firm rely on its usual internal general counsel or outside attorney to negotiate contracts against highly experienced and aggressive attorneys representing private equity buyers. The sellers typically lost 5 percent to 15 percent of the negotiated purchase price through unfavorable escrows, contingent liabilities, and obligations contained in the final contract. Sellers' attorneys were smart and talented, but in each case they had never been involved in such a significant transaction.

Senior People

In interviewing prospective advisors, it's imperative for you to assure that people pitching their services will be the people advising you. You want the senior, veteran experts consulting on your transaction, not their junior associates. Your due diligence in selecting advisors includes not only interviewing them personally but seeking referrals and references from their former clients, other businesses in your industry, and your personal network. In seeking references who can advise about the advisor, ask about sales that have been similar, their outcome, the advisor's responsiveness, and quality of insight and strategy.

Ask your candidates the hard questions, and dig deep for answers. Some investment bankers will provide you a proposal that shows pages of "tombstones" with names in your industry, to persuade you that they have conducted numerous sales like yours. Be sure to have them specifically identify which of these companies they actually served as the lead banking firm on a sale, as opposed to having performed a valuation, or obtained financing.

Commitment and Fit

Ability is critical, but—again—so is a good fit of personalities and organizational cultures. Advisors will be with you through stressful strategizing, complex negotiations, and temporary setbacks. You and your teams need to feel sufficiently comfortable with one another to ask questions, debate, and discuss issues openly. Advisors are expected to be available around the clock. Deal negotiations do not respect office hours.

Fees

Good advisors will be expensive, but their skills are invaluable in generating interest, achieving an optimum sale price, and constructing a clean, favorable deal that closes on time. Their long experience in doing repeatedly what you will only do once in a lifetime is truly priceless for you. Try to negotiate a reasonable fee per hour with your attorneys, but understand that their experience and time, albeit expensive, will inure to your financial benefit in the end. In negotiating fees with investment bankers, structure their incentives so that capturing a higher price will earn them more. Aligning the best interests of the banker with yours produces the best outcome for all.

Conclusion

Preparing your company for sale, preparing the requisite documents, selecting your sale strategy, and engaging in the multitude of endless activities and decisions involved in this undertaking will not be a one-person job. You need your most trusted internal advisors and a team of competent, veteran external advisors to help you through to a successful sale. And their involvement needs to begin early. You'll find that you don't need the full team for every session, but convene your complete team at the outset. Then identify the core team that you will be in constant contact with and will meet with at least weekly. The sale of your business begins with a goal, but its conclusion is never guaranteed. You can ramp up the odds of a superb success by carefully choosing and assembling your professional advisors. Your team may be the key to fully accomplishing your objectives. Assuring the best result is more assured, however, if you have the best people in your corner.

Takeaway Lessons

- Selling a business requires the best team of experts you can assemble, and many of them are already on your payroll. The lawyers, accountants, and managers who helped make your business successful are the first you should involve in selling it. Their familiarity with you and your operations will be essential in preparing documents and negotiating your sale.
- It will be impossible to conduct and conclude your sale without the help of external advisors, especially an investment banker, a transaction attorney, and an external auditor. These professionals help you frame and carry out the selling process. They will also prepare the documents that legal requirements impose and potential buyers will require.
- In selecting external advisory, you want experienced senior people who are compatible with you and your selling team. You should insist that the high-profile execs who pitch their firms' advisors services are the people assigned to your sale. You want advisors whose savvy equals that of your buyer's advisors, especially if you are selling your firm to a larger firm or a private equity fund with a history of acquisitions.
- Your advisory team needs to include a personal financial counselor and an estate planner who can guide you in creating trusts and family financial arrangements after the sale. When necessary, consider bringing in advisors who specialize in specific situations, such as, for instance, helping you and family members resolve reservations and disagreements that affect your sale.

For additional resources and tools, visit www.sellingyourbusinessformore.com

CHAPTER 8

Considering Alternatives: Special Situations

Introduction

Every sale of a business is special, if only because it's a major life event for the seller. As you've seen in earlier chapters, every sale has negotiations and issues and sticking points that make it unlike comparable transactions. But there are several types of sale transactions that qualify for the term "special" as a group. We'll discuss four of the most frequently seen situations in this chapter, although a full list would be much longer.

The first special situation is that in which a business has multiple owners. We noted earlier that having multiple owners often complicates any potential sale. Some shareholders (if the firm is a corporation) or partners (if it's organized another way) may be at different stages in life, may have financial or family issues, or may have differing ideas about the business. From the moment a co-owner raises the possibility of selling, these differences may create discord, and they certainly will raise questions that must be answered—whether to sell all of the business or part, who remains involved in the firm when others sell out, how payments are structured, and many others.

Another frequently seen special situation is the departure of a founder. For any number of reasons, the gray eminence of the firm—whose name may be on the door, whose personality shaped the business, the person who in some ways *is* the business—decides to leave. This sudden vacuum in ownership at the top needs to be filled by new owners.

The third special situation is potentially a happy one: someone—a competitor, a business seeking to diversify, a private equity player—shows up out of the blue with an offer to buy your company. You need guidelines for evaluating an unexpected offer. A first offer may not be your best offer, and an external sale may not be your optimal first choice.

We won't discuss the final type of "special" situation extensively, but keep it in mind throughout your reading and as a consideration in deciding to sell your business. However prosperous your firm is or however like-minded your co-owners or partners are, stuff happens. Economies sour, business cycles turn down, M and A activity wanes, lenders dry up, and industries re-rationalize or disappear. Each of these possibilities can make it difficult to sell your business to another firm or private equity buyer. When sale to an external buyer is unlikely, you need alternatives.

If you find yourself in any of those situations, this chapter will help.

Multiple Owners

Thus far, we've generally presumed that a single owner is selling a business. Sometimes, however, several shareholders own a business. They may be spouses, parents and children, unrelated business partners, or a combination of people, trusts, and charities. As difficult as it is for you alone to decide to sell your business, getting multiple partners on board such a life-changing determination is no easy task. Each owner will have his or her own personal agenda about continued employment, a distinct family financial picture, and degrees of emotional attachment to the firm.

Raising the Idea of Selling

Every sale of a multi-owner business begins with one owner bringing up the topic. If you're that person, be as factual and objective as possible in raising the subject, and explain clearly and simply why you're interested in selling. Selling a business is an emotional undertaking, so don't pile any unnecessary drama atop it.

Perhaps you have personal reasons for suggesting the business be sold—your need for liquidity, illness, a wish to retire. This is the time to explain them and to ask your co-owners to understand your position.

You may feel that relationships within the ownership group are becoming dysfunctional, and you want to sell before anger and acrimony take over entirely. For example, do you see intractable succession issues when the generation in power retires? Is one owner unwilling to risk additional capital to lift the firm to its next level? Have other owners confided they'd like to take money off the table?

Genuine business concerns may motivate you to suggest selling. For instance, your industry may be changing in ways that will cost your company its competitive edge and sale value. You may anticipate the economy, or business cycle won't favor a sale if you wait. Conversely, firms in your industry recently may have sold at attractive prices, and you believe you and the other owners should take advantage of the current favorable market.

If you aren't the one who initially raises the issue of selling, act as if you were. Show your co-owner the courtesy, objectivity, and rationality you'd expect in his or her position. Listen first, speak later. Remember, a sale that separates any owner from a company is more than a transaction. It's a major shift in the life of each owner, and that fact will play heavily in each owner's reaction to selling.

Continuing the Discussion

Regardless of who initiates discussion of a sale, the next step is to seek agreement among most or all owners that exploring a sale is worthwhile. Again, let reason and objectivity prevail. Counselors who consult business owners on succession and transition can facilitate everyone's thinking, discussion, and decision; it might be worthwhile to bring them in.

Once the group agrees to entertain a sale, the process is similar to that involving a single owner. In fact, some activities will be completely independent of your co-owners—for example, reviewing your family financial plan, wills, and estate in light of a future sale of the business. But other actions will require convening the group, because each person will have opinions about the value, objectives, and future of the company.

Achieve a consensus on priorities. Would some people like to remain with the company after selling, and, if so, in what role? Do others prefer to cash out and separate? Is everyone in accord about retaining employees and as many jobs and benefits as possible? Is there consensus about the risk you're all willing to take or, conversely, the opportunity you wish to retain—for instance, offering to finance a potential buyer or insisting on full payment at closing without further risk or opportunity?

If there's serious dissonance about whether selling right away is the best decision, hire an investment bank to provide alternatives. It can suggest timing and strategies and predict their relative outcomes. The investment banker can even discuss qualitative advantages and disadvantages of each strategy as they affect owners, management, employees, and other stakeholders. An investment banker's analysis will provide ranges of value among reasonable choices for proceeding with a sale now as compared to building out the business for some number of years in the future and selling then, based on consistent assumptions. Consequently, the group will have analytical data to discuss and evaluate as they debate a sale.

Assemble the Selling Team

When the group has reached general agreement—or at least mutual understanding—it's time to construct the selling team. Make it a group exercise to interview investment banks and decide which you will invite to give proposals. Let everyone participate in on-site interviews with finalists. But name a quarterback from your group so it's clear who's responsible for moving the process forward and who will be group spokesman to advisors and candidates for the advisory team.

Moving Toward Sale

As the selling process reaches the stage of letters of intent or purchase and sale contracts, the group should determine if one or a few members will be authorized to sign documents. The full group needs to deliberate and agree on who will review proposals and documents as they are drafted—besides attorneys, accountants, bankers, and the CFO on the deal team. The process runs more efficiently if one or two owners assume responsibility for review, feedback, and approval of important documents.

Regular communication of developments to the deal team and owners during planning and marketing makes for smooth execution. We find that a weekly update meeting provides a forum for those active in the marketing and negotiating to communicate their progress and for the other stakeholders to get questions answered and participate in shaping the unfolding process.

Sale by a Few Owners

Sometimes your situation won't be as clear-cut as you and your co-owners deciding as a group to sell an entire company. Consider the following scenarios:

- Scenario One: Some owners of the business want to cash out their equity while others want to continue owning and operating the business.
- Scenario Two: One or more owners having a substantial portion of their wealth in the business would like to take some money off the table.
- Scenario Three: One or more owners agree now is the time to sell the business, but they'd like to retain an equity interest in it. They may also want to remain involved in managing or operating it at some level.

When any of these situations arise, you need alternatives to an outright sale of the whole business, alternatives that accommodate needs of one or two owners. We'll look at two available options to incorporated businesses. The first is selling stock to an Employee Stock Ownership Plan. The second is sale and recapitalization of the corporation.

Sale of Stock to an Employee Stock Ownership Plan

In situations like Scenario One and Scenario Two, consider creating an Employee Stock Ownership Plan (ESOP) for your incorporated business.

An ESOP is an employer-sponsored benefit through which employees own shares in the corporation they work for. Although a full explanation of the types of ESOPs and their workings would be exceedingly involved, the concept is straightforward. The corporation sets up a trust to which it contributes shares of its stock or cash with which to buy its shares. As a general rule, all full-time employees over age twenty-one may participate in an ESOP. Through a formula based upon their salary and perhaps other considerations, the corporation allocates shares in the ESOP trust—called a *beneficial interest*—to each participating employee. Employees accrue actual ownership of stock held by the ESOP—they become *vested*, gradually or all at once—over a specified interval that they must remain with the corporation. When employees depart after vesting, they receive their stock, which the corporation buys from them at an appraised price (if the corporation isn't publicly traded) or the market price (if the corporation's stock is listed on an exchange).

For Scenarios One and Two, there's an immediate advantage in creating an ESOP: some owners could sell their stock to the ESOP and receive cash without affecting other owners. But there may also be advantages to your corporation. When employees are shareholders, they benefit twofold from their contribution to the business—they earn a salary as workers, and as owners they participate personally in its growing value. Thus, creating an ESOP might inspire employee commitment to the company's success and growth.

Funding an ESOP

A corporation that establishes an ESOP must acquire the stock to fund it. To do so, the corporation typically borrows money from a bank or other well-heeled lender, and, in turn, it lends that money to the ESOP. The ESOP buys the stock—in Scenarios One and Two, from a selling shareholder—at fair market value as determined by an independent appraiser and confirmed by the ESOP's trustee. Stock the ESOP acquires must, in general, be voting common stock. In addition, ESOP stock will carry voting and dividend rights senior to any class of common stock or convertible preferred. Thereafter, the corporation contributes to the ESOP for purposes of repaying the company's loan.

Example of a Leveraged ESOP Transaction

The flowchart below exhibits the basic attributes of a leveraged ESOP transaction, which utilizes bank financing (see figure 8.1).

First, the Employer Corp., which has 30,000 outstanding shares of common voting stock, borrows $10 million from a bank and then lends that $10 million to the new Employer Corp ESOP Trust. The ESOP in turn purchases 10,000 shares from the selling shareholders at the FMV value of $1,000 per share for a total purchase price of $10 million. The selling shareholders invest the proceeds in Qualified Replacement Property as a "1042 rollover," named for the provision in tax law that permits this transaction.

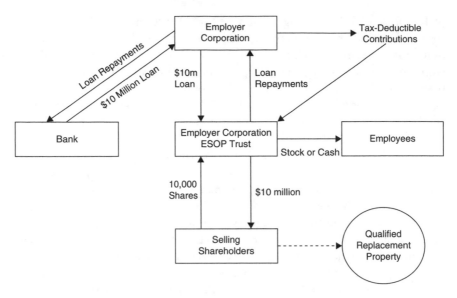

Figure 8.1   Leveraged ESOP

The ESOP initially holds the acquired stock in a suspense account. Each year, shares are released as loan repayments are made, and the released shares are allocated to the accounts of the eligible participants. Employer Corp. makes annual contributions to the ESOP to fund the ESOP loan repayment. The ESOP makes annual loan repayments to Employer Corp., and Employer Corp. makes annual loan payments back to the bank. As employees retire they can exercise a "put" option to convert their stock to cash.

Usually the annual allocation of shares is made based on the relative salaries of the participants. The ESOP is the shareholder of all the stock held in the ESOP. The ESOP trustee votes the stock on routine matters, but for nonpublic corporations, participants may have limited pass-through voting rights on major events such as mergers, acquisitions, and sale of materially all the assets of the corporation.

Tax Advantages

Although limitations are complex and beyond our discussion, a leveraged ESOP transaction offers the corporation significant tax advantages. Specifically, its contributions to the ESOP and dividends it pays on stock held in the ESOP are tax deductible.

In addition, sellers in Scenarios One and Two may enjoy tax advantages if stock they sell to the ESOP is stock of a Chapter C corporation. Specifically, they may be able to defer indefinitely tax on capital gains generated by the sale. In some cases, they may eliminate owing taxes on those gains.

Let's assume that sellers in Scenarios One and Two own voting common stock in a Chapter C corporation. In addition, they are able and willing to sell to the ESOP in a single, integrated transaction. That sale results in the ESOP owning 30 percent of the corporation on a *fully diluted basis*. That is, the amount of stock would represent 30 percent ownership of the corporation if all other "equity equivalents," such as convertible debentures, were converted to common stock.

Under Internal Revenue Code Section 1042, taxable gains on sale of their stock to the ESOP may be deferred if the sellers reinvest an amount equal to the proceeds of their sale in qualified replacement property. Further, sellers in Scenarios One and Two must purchase the qualified replacement property during the period three months before to twelve months after the date they sold their stock to the ESOP. That period is in effect whether sellers were paid in a lump sum or in installments. When sellers meet the IRS requirements and purchase the qualified replacement property, the tax cost basis of the C corporation stock sold will carry over to the newly purchased property.

If they later sell the qualified replacement property, they must pay taxes on its capital gains. However, a special consideration applies if the seller has died and his estate is disposing of the qualified replacement property. In this case, its cost basis will be "stepped up" to its value at the time of death. Capital gains tax will then effectively have been eliminated.

"Qualified replacement property" is a term with a cumbersome definition. It consists of common or preferred stocks, bonds, and debt issued by a publicly traded or closely held domestic corporation. That corporation must employ at least half of its assets in an active trade or business. And its passive investment income for the preceding year—the sum of interest, dividends, capital gains, royalties the corporation earns—cannot exceed 25 percent of its gross revenues. Some leveraged investments also meet the definition of qualified replacement property, allowing sellers greater flexibility in choices.

Under the circumstances outlined, the selling owners in Scenarios One and Two will have a buyer for their minority interest that would most likely not otherwise exist. Assuming they reinvest in qualified replacement property, they also will defer or eliminate taxes on the resultant capital gains.

Exception for Subchapter S Corporations

However, if the corporation is a Subchapter S corporation—not a Chapter C corporation—tax advantages of selling stock to the ESOP that we have previously outlined disappear. Sellers in Scenarios One and Two will not enjoy deferral of capital gains on stock sold to the ESOP. Advantages granted by Internal Revenue Code Section 1042 don't apply to them. However, there is one important tax advantage available to the S-Corp itself: the ESOP trust itself is not subject to income tax. Consequently, the portion of the S-Corp income that would be passed through to the ESOP by virtue of its ownership of shares will not be subject to any income tax.

Sellers may have received tax advantages from owning stock in a Subchapter S corporation—for instance, they didn't pay corporate tax rates—and that may have to be benefit enough: selling the entire company is their only alternative to raise the cash they desire in Scenarios One and Two.

Disadvantages of an ESOP

If a sale to an ESOP has so many advantages, why isn't this alternative more widely used? Some of the major reasons are:

- Creating an ESOP, administering it, and securing its tax advantages are complex undertakings.
- Not all business owners want their employees as co-owners with some level of control over the business.
- Debt levels, cash flows, employees' ages, timing, costs of repurchase and diversification requirements, and the employee salary base might make an ESOP infeasible.
- Substantial excise taxes apply to some dispositions of ESOP stock. These tax considerations could alter the timing of the firm's eventual sale to an outside buyer, or they could at least be a factor in sale negotiations and price.
- The fiduciary duties owed the employee beneficiaries of the ESOP may conflict with the goals and objectives of the non-ESOP shareholders.
- If you sell your stock to an ESOP, the price you receive likely will be less per share than the price you'd receive by selling the entire company.

Creating an ESOP clearly is not suitable for every company or co-owner wishing to sell stock to it. Even though the ESOP can be an effective solution to Scenarios One and Two, owners shouldn't rush into creating one. You and your co-owners need to have competent advisors for a feasibility study.

Two final notes of caution are warranted. Shareholders who sell stock to the ESOP must be cautious about the number of shares they sell and the timing of their sales. Otherwise, they can inadvertently transfer an unacceptable level of control to the ESOP or suffer the loss of a controlling premium on the stock they retain. Also, it's difficult to anticipate how a later buyer of the entire company might view an ESOP. Its existence might dissuade a potential buyer or prompt him to insist on restrictive terms and a lower sale price.

Sale and Recapitalization of a Corporation

Broadly defined, *recapitalization* is the process of changing a firm's capital structure by altering the mix of debt and equity on its balance sheet without changing the total amount of capital. A *sale and recapitalization*, or "sale and recap," involves carrying out that process as part of a change in ownership. A sale and recap is one method you might pursue to meet the objectives of Scenario Three.

Example of Sale and Recap

To understand how this alternative might work, consider the following situation:

Retailers, Inc., sells gadgets in locations nationwide. Its capital structure contains one class of stock—voting common stock. Bob Seller, the company's CEO, owns 40 percent of those outstanding shares. Dave Seller, chairman of the board, owns 40 percent. Fran Seller, VP of Operations, owns 20 percent.

Retailers, Inc. has had rapid growth in earnings over the past few years and forecasts dramatic growth after entering new markets. Therefore, the Sellers decided to investigate the market for their company.

For this purpose, they hired an investment banker, making it clear they wanted an optimal sales price paid mostly in cash, and that one or more of them wanted to stay with the company after sale. Their investment banker located a private equity partnership that agreed to the Sellers' price and continued involvement in the business. It proposed the following transaction:

- The private equity partnership would acquire 13 percent of Retailers' outstanding shares through a tax-free exchange. That exchange would be comprised of common stock, 10 percent junior preferred stock, and 10 percent senior preferred stock of Newco Retailers, Inc., having a value equal to 13 percent of the total purchase price.
- Newco Retailers would acquire 87 percent of Retail, Inc.'s outstanding shares for cash equal to 87 percent of the purchase price. This cash would be funded through the capital contribution of the private equity partnership and by issuing other debt and equity.
- At closing, all parties would enter into a shareholders agreement covering all issued shares. The agreement included rights for the Sellers to participate in any future public offering from Newco Retailers.
- Bob Sellers would receive a five-year employment agreement during which time he would remain CEO and groom a chosen successor to take over in five years.
- David and Fran Sellers had no desire to continue with the company. They received a severance package.

Illustration

The flowchart in figure 8.2 exhibits the basic attributes of the proposed transaction.

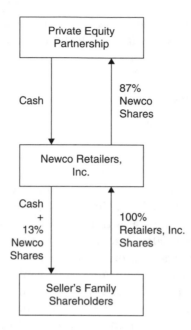

Figure 8.2 Sale and Recap

The offer provided no guaranteed exit strategy for the Sellers' equity interests in Newco Retailers, Inc., but the private equity partnership projected an exit opportunity via Newco's initial public offering in four to seven years.

This offer met the criteria the Sellers specified to their investment banker. They received their requested price, albeit with some risk associated with retaining equity interest in Newco. However, that risk also represented opportunity to recognize some of the upside they projected for Newco after acquiring Retail, Inc. Bob Sellers remained in the management of the company and had the opportunity to groom his successor.

In sum, this hypothetical sale and recapitalization achieved the objectives laid out in Scenario Three.

Other Uses of Sale and Recap

A sale and recap of Retail, Inc. might also serve the goals of Scenarios One and Two. For example, let's say that Fran was the only Seller interested in cutting all ties to Retail, Inc., and Bob and Dave are willing to accept the arrangement offered by the acquiring private equity group. In this case, the deal could have been restructured to provide Fran an all-cash buyout with Bob and Dave receiving a greater portion of the purchase price through the tax-free exchange of stock. Of course, it's hard to say if a sale and recap could be structured along such lines while earning an optimal sale price.

Management Buyout

A *management buyout* (MBO) is the sale of a firm to its current executives and managers. Although there are many instances in which an MBO is attractive, one common instance is the departure of a company's founder.

Reasons for an MBO

There are at least two reasons a founder might consider selling his business to his management team—loyalty to the managers and limited alternatives for an outside sale. Having built a company from the ground up, founders of successful businesses often have strong loyalties to their executive team, especially if those men and women were part of the firm's founding. If the executives are younger than the founder and are interested in continuing the firm, the owner at a minimum may feel obligated to consider this alternative, rather than sell the company to strangers. Since the executive team will likely keep loyal employees on board, the founder who values employee retention will realize an added benefit. And in slow merger and acquisition cycles, some companies won't attract outside buyers and a marketing effort may seem fruitless. An interested management team may offer the founder the only feasible exit solution.

Valuation

The valuation of a firm entering an MBO will be comparable to the price fetched from a purely financial buyer. There likely will be no strategic premium, since the company will continue to run much as-is with no overt synergies following transfer of ownership. Usually, management lacks adequate capital or access to financing to pay significant cash at closing, so the MBO often will be an installment sale or earn-out. The founder's payout is, therefore, completely dependent on the continued success of the business over the period of the installment sale or earn-out.

Questions to Consider

Before entering an MBO deal, consider these questions:

- Is your business technology-based—for instance, an internet infrastructure provider? Technology-based businesses demand continued refinement, development of new technology and products, and adroit management in an ever-changing industry. Or is your business model more stable and established—for example, metal fabricating? Stable, established businesses need sound management skills and leadership, but perhaps not such sweeping vision and innovation.
- Does your management group have the skills and characteristics to steward your company and grow it? Is there an obvious choice for CEO? If you

have been the dominant salesman, how will your departure affect sales and revenues?

- Is there a board of directors, or at least an advisory board, to assist management during the transition and thereafter?

Caveat Vendor

If you're considering "exit by MBO," you need to be financially secure personally before considering sale. There likely won't be a substantial cash payment at closing, so you must be sure your future financial needs are satisfied. At the least, you must have a personal financial cushion in case your successors delay payments or your earn-out is less than forecast.

The Offer You Can't Refuse—Or Is It?

Let's say you receive a letter from the CEO of a competitor stating he wants to offer $200 million for your commercial real estate development business. The last time you had any formal indication of your company's value was three years ago, when you gave stock to your children. Then your company's appraised enterprise value was $100 million. You are fifty-eight years old and had always expected to work into your mid-sixties and perhaps pass your business to your three children. What do you do?

A Credible Buyer, But...

If the prospective buyer is credible, take the offer seriously. But consider what might have prompted this interest. Is the buyer hoping to exploit a perceived vulnerability in your ownership? Does the buyer seem to have a particular strategic purpose? Has a key executive or manager of your firm resigned? If your firm has multiple owners, has any gossiped about disputes affecting the company?

If there's been a death, illness, or disruption among owners, suspect a bottom-feeder who is trying to take advantage of a situation. Even if the valuation seems appealing, expect that any further negotiation and due diligence will bring significant downward repricing. If there are no adverse circumstances in your company or ownership, is there any evidence or speculation that the competitor has been seeking acquisitions with strategic advantages? Are there synergies if your firms were to combine?

A Reason Not to Sell?

Bring the inquiry to the attention of other owners and to the board of directors; they should be involved in deciding whether to pursue the initiative. There may be reasons that obviate any consideration of selling just now. Perhaps you have entered a joint venture with a high-end mall developer that will exponentiate your reputation and enlarge your corporate footprint. Perhaps your son just received his MBA from Wharton and has joined your business hoping to make it his career. For whatever reason, you know you're not ready to step away from the successful business you built at any price.

Thinking It Over

But if it isn't clear that now is no time to sell, start evaluating the offer. For one thing, you don't know what your business is worth today, and therefore don't know if the offer is as generous as it seems. If a sale is in the offing, you might better pursue a more formal sale process than negotiate with a single buyer. You should examine what values and cultural objectives you want in a successful sale and whether the competitor meets them. If you'd like a continuing role in your company after an acquisition, how would you design it and would this company's management be amenable to your preferences?

Ascertain Value

If the direction of your business is well established, hire a valuation expert to assess your firm's appeal to both a financial buyer and a synergistic or strategic buyer. This report will set a reasonable expectation for ranges of value and give you a basis with which to compare the offer and to negotiate.

Maybe your business is at an inflexion point. Perhaps you and your management have been struggling over which of several growth initiatives to pursue or perhaps you've discussed whether to seek a sale. Now is the time to resolve that stalemate. Bring in an investment banker with experience in commercial real estate for an objective view of your strategic alternatives. You may find that a particular strategy or combination of initiatives will bring substantially more in the future than the competitor is offering today. Or you may just ascertain a range of value that will give you some teeth in negotiating a final price.

Whether to Seek More Buyers

If, after all that, the price still seems attractive, ask your investment banker what is happening in the M and A market for your industry. You have the greatest opportunity for an optimum price when there are many competing bids, so you should ask whether the transaction environment is favorable. Despite their grumblings to the contrary, buyers who approach you likely will remain bidders when other buyers are interested. Some may refuse to participate in a broad auction, but most are willing to compete against a few buyers.

Examine Values

Consider the qualitative aspects of a potential sale. Is the culture of this competitor similar to the culture you instilled in your firm? Will your employees be treated well and maintain their salary and benefits? Do you need to consider implications in your community?

Can You Remain?

What about a continued role for you? Would you like to be part of the ongoing business, or would you rather take your money and move on? Would this firm be the right match for you? If you contemplate a management role for a period of time, how would your responsibilities change? If the acquirer is a public company, management decisions will emphasize quarterly reporting, and inclinations to invest in long-term initiatives may be deflected. Even as manager of a division, you'll no longer be the sole decision maker. You'll have to persuade a more senior officer that every suggestion has merit and secure approval to undertake major efforts. Such an environment may not be agreeable.

Conclusion

Many factors demand your attention if special considerations pertain to selling your business. If more than one person owns your business, certainly issues of tact and consideration arise alongside the need for cold-eyed business judgment. If you're a founder parting with a life's work or a hardworking owner who's received an offer you never expected, your situation embodies a combination of sentiment and savvy not to be underestimated.

The issues are special, and so are your alternatives. Whether they're creating an ESOP, agreeing to an MBO, or a simply answering "Maybe" to a good deal, each will have advantages, disadvantages, and implications. Sorting through these issues and talking with other owners, directors, and advisors will help you make the right choices.

Takeaway Lessons

- Selling your business may present a series of singular dilemmas. In the case of multiple owners, you may have to overcome resistance to the sale and accommodate the differing needs your co-owners bring to the proposition. In such cases, you're not only negotiating with a prospective buyer, you're striving for accord within your personal and business family, and the effort likely will persist through every stage in the selling process. Courtesy and consideration are essential tools for doing so.
- When selling is a group enterprise, you want to establish a balance of involvement and authority. Perhaps, for instance, everyone should be present

to interview candidates to hire as investment bankers, but you'll want to appoint one or two owners to sign documents and provide approvals as representatives of all owners.

- Special circumstances—such as the retirement of a founder or conflicting needs of co-owners—call for specialized solutions. When selling in a conventional transaction is unfeasible, an increasingly popular alternative is selling your firm to an ESOP. Besides selling your business to your employees through an ESOP, you might consider selling it to your managers via an MBO, and you might also investigate selling through a recapitalization. Each of these can be an alternative to irascible markets and the solution for a special situation.

- Receiving a bid out of the blue for your business is both pleasant and perplexing. And if you hadn't previously thought about selling, the unsolicited offer jolts you into considering it. You need to assess the buyer's credibility and his motivations, but you also need to initiate many of the actions you'd take if you had decided to sell—determining your company's realistic valuation, for instance, or deciding whether to seek more bidders. The moment you entertained the thought of accepting an offer, you entered some aspect of the sale process, even if you later decide to decline.

For additional resources and tools, visit www.sellingyourbusinessformore.com

CHAPTER 9

Timing Is Everything:
Pulling the Trigger

Introduction

When is the right time to bring a company to the market? Should you wait until merger and acquisition activity nears the top of the cycle? Are there ever reasons to bring your company to market in a slow M and A environment? If you can't find the right buyer—or any buyer—which alternatives should you consider for selling your company? The answer is, "It depends." It depends on the nature of your business, your motive to sell, circumstances specific to your situation, and events in your business's sector or industry.

Motives for Selling

Motivations to sell vary broadly. For example, a life event—yours or a loved one's—may trigger thoughts of selling a business. Favorable market and economic conditions may prompt you to consider a sale—for instance, obvious consolidation in your industry, active interest from a buyer, a robust economy, or recent sale of a competitor at a high price. Perhaps you may consider selling to take advantage of another business opportunity. Or "It's just time to sell and move on." There are as many motives to sell a business as the human condition can present.

Every motivation to sell has a psychological companion: a degree of urgency. The owner who would like to retire "someday soon" brings one degree of urgency to selling his business. The owner who's had a life-threatening heart attack brings quite another. If a business owner has died with no succession plan or evident successor, the urgency is absolute and immediate. Heirs or creditors may force an immediate sale to discharge indebtedness or to provide for estate taxes, inheritances, and gifts for charity.

But there is another master to be considered in making the decision to sell, the arbiter of many business and financial decisions, the market—in this case, the market for mergers and acquisitions (M and A) in which sellers and buyers meet.

Characteristics of Strong M and A Markets

From your perspective, a strong M and A market is one that features many buyers, availability of cash, reasonable access to credit, and a positive business cycle. Consolidation in an industry is another indicator of strong markets for sellers in that industry, and exchange rate fluctuations can increase the number of foreign buyers for a seller's company.

The more of these factors that are present, the better will be the market for you as a prospective seller. In 2006 through the first half of 2008, most of these factors coalesced to generate a frothy M and A market, and sellers quickly and easily received high multiples of cash flow for their companies.

Many Buyers

The first characteristic that defines a strong market for selling a business is the presence of many buyers seeking acquisitions and willing to pay a sizable price for the right company. A greater number of active, interested buyers seeking companies like yours also enlarge the likelihood of completing a sale, and competition among buyers raises the prospect of your sale fetching the highest price.

The strongest M and A markets feature both *strategic buyers* and *financial buyers*.

Strategic Buyers
Strategic buyers are firms in their prospective acquisition's business or a related business. They hope to realize good returns on investment through synergies created when a purchased company is integrated into theirs. Examples of synergistic strategies include:

- Acquiring a company in the strategic buyer's supply chain to streamline costs
- Purchasing a company whose product can be added to the buyer's distribution network
- Acquiring a competitor in markets the acquirer hasn't penetrated
- A strategic buyer acquiring a competitor with production facilities or distribution networks that fill in its expansion plan

Financial Buyers
Financial buyers are entrepreneurial investors pursuing a transaction for its reasonable rate of return. They view the purchase as an investment, not as an

extension of their operating vision. Most prevalent among financial buyers are the numerous private equity funds that make acquisitions on behalf of their investors. These funds accept money from investors, largely institutional investors like pension funds and foundations as well as wealthy individuals and families, which they in turn invest directly in private companies. Investors expect to get a substantial return on their investment within the ten-year or twelve-year term of the fund agreement.

Private equity firms invest their capital by buying stock of private companies, usually purchasing the whole company or at least the controlling interest in the company. The funds' strategy for generating a return to their investors and to themselves is to find, buy, and grow companies so they can then sell them at a substantial profit or in some cases bring them public within the time constraints of their agreement. These funds are committed to realizing a targeted return on investment within the terms of their agreement with investors. They are also bound by their agreement with investors to invest the capital they have accumulated within a period of up to five or six years from the onset of the funds. If they do not invest the capital within that time frame, they are obligated to return it to investors. No fund manager wants to do that.

Their customary strategy is to acquire small but well-performing platform businesses in a particular industry and grow it through further acquisitions in the same industry. A fund implementing such a strategy will be a hybrid of financial and strategic buyer, and the fund will be willing to pay some element of a strategic premium. Also, if a particular fund's investment horizon is nearing with capital remaining uninvested, fund managers may become aggressive in offering a seller more favorable pricing.

Private equity funds have differing strategies and characteristics. Some funds employ deal managers involved with day-to-day management and strategic decisions of companies they acquire. Others rely on the acquired company's operating managers to run the business and oversee their investment from the board of directors.

Available Cash Balances

Another characteristic of a strong M and A market—that is, one favoring sellers—is copious cash on prospective buyers' balance sheets or in coffers of private equity funds. Substantial cash positions are favorable to sellers for several reasons. First, the opportunity cost of cash is generally high. Excluding periods like the late 1970s, when interest rates on cash balances reached double digits, cash earns a higher return when invested in other assets. Second, shareholders of corporations and investors in equity funds don't pay managers to hold cash; they expect their capital to be deployed more productively. Third, plentiful cash balances enable equity financing, granting prospective buyers flexibility in structuring deals.

Access to Financing

Buyers usually employ some leverage to boost their returns, however. Therefore, easy access to credit at attractive terms is another defining feature of a favorable M and A market.

Positive Business Cycle

Similarly, a prosperous business cycle, evidenced by earnings growth, begets an active M and A market. Potential buyers will be more confident of a good investment return if they see growing demand and expansion in their industry.

Weakening Dollar

Weak or weakening exchange rates for the U.S. dollar make markets favorable for a sale. A relatively weak dollar may prompt foreign buyers to seek U.S. acquisitions because U.S. firms will seem cheap compared to comparable firms in their own country. Also, increasing demand in their countries for U.S. goods—another consequence of a weaker dollar—will increase their appetite to acquire U.S. companies producing them.

Industry Consolidation

Some industries normally are comprised of small local or regional firms. As markets change and expand through developments in technology, transportation, and distribution, many such industries get consolidated through acquisition by regional, national, or even global firms. When consolidation is taking place in an industry, its best performers have a seller's advantage.

Supply in a Strong Market

Not all characteristics of strong markets involve buyers' demand for a sagacious acquisition. On the supply side, owners who built their firms from the ground up and have a low cost basis have more incentives to sell than owners of firms still working off start-up costs. Thus, presence of long-term owners who have greater equity in their businesses—equity that becomes cash if the company is sold—contributes to a favorable market.

Other things being equal, they will be more motivated to tap that equity if capital gains tax rates are inviting, especially if there's a high probability that tax rates will increase. Thus, current and prospective tax considerations also influence the supply of businesses offered in strong markets. In addition, current and potential regulatory and legislative issues increase—or decrease—the supply of companies on the market.

Characteristics of Weak M and A Markets

Not surprisingly, a weak M and A market will have attributes opposite those of a strong market.

- Fewer domestic buyers are in the market.
- Capital markets are tight, and it is difficult to obtain credit for an acquisition without high interest rates and strict covenants.
- Even where credit is available, dollar limits are cyclically low.
- A poor business cycle dampens confidence that new investment will generate required returns.
- A strong U.S. dollar discourages foreign buyers from U.S. acquisitions, reducing the buyer pool and competition among buyers.

The period surrounding the severe global recession beginning mid-2007 was a stunning example of a weak M and A market. Every adversity listed above was evident during that time. It is important to note, however, that even in weak business cycles, subsets of some industries will attract buyers at favorable prices. During the recession of 2007, the healthcare sector performed well and drew buyers willing to pay handsomely for firms. Also in that period, strategic buyers with adequate cash acquired high-performance companies with valuations under $75 million, mainly in equity deals. In sum, poor economies and weak M and A markets don't inevitably mean "No Sale."

Deciding Whether to Sell and When

The three components of a decision to sell—motivation, urgency, and markets—are now in place. If you are considering sale of your company, what should you do?

First, whatever your motivation may be, you need to understand it and its degree of urgency, and you need to consider a time horizon for selling. Do extenuating circumstances or strong preferences insist that your business be sold? If so, how quickly? This year? Or are you interested in selling but content to wait several years?

Second, you should assess your business's recent results and its forecasts for the next several years. Ideally, earnings are trending up, and your company is ready for sale whenever you wish. A hard look at competitors is useful. You need to gauge your company's singular strengths and differentiators and whether they will persist. You should examine trends in your industry to see if consolidation is taking place or is likely during your window of opportunity, or if there are other pressing factors pertinent to demand for the company. If you are years from selling, a business consultant can help formulate this analysis. If your sale is within a year, an investment banker will complete it as a first step.

Third, you should examine the current and prospective macro-economies and anticipate the M and A market that likely will attend them. Market cycles ebb and flow. Although economic history offers insight into the duration of business cycles, it's perilous to assume a good market will continue or a poor market will revive in a year or two. By the same token, it's unreasonable to believe economies and markets will never survive any present moment's adversities.

Realistic expectations are vital in any cycle, but particularly in the trough of a business cycle, and especially if you need to sell your business. After a boom M and A cycle such as 2006 and 2007, when transactions in some industries fetched twelve- and thirteen-times cash flow, lower multiples seem pedestrian. However, lower multiples may be normal and reasonable for the industry, especially viewed over a cycle of ten to fifteen years. Holding out for extreme valuations probably will not be fruitful.

Unless your company has particular appeal, marketing and selling your business will take longer in a slow business cycle. From launching the effort to close, a time lapse of twelve to eighteen months is quite possible and to be expected.

The best time to sell your business, of course, is when the business, the economy, and the M and A market are strong. However, going to market then may feel wrong to you. After all, it is counterintuitive to pick the blossom when the rose is blooming. That sense of well-being may breed indecision. A seller who betrays lack of conviction will dissuade buyers, especially private equity firms, who will simply move on to the next deal, taking your opportunity with them. Other buyers may hang on longer to bring a deal together, but your indecision may curtail any negotiating advantage. Therefore, the first rule of deciding to sell your business is *Decide to Sell Your Business* (see figure 9.1).

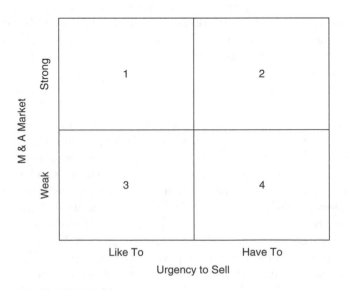

Figure 9.1   The Decision Matrix

The Decision Matrix

Business practitioners and students doubtless have encountered the decision matrix in figure 9.1, and it's useful in picturing the three elements of a seller's decision to place his or her company on the market. The vertical left axis represents the M and A environment—strong or weak. The horizontal axis represents the urgency of your motive to sell, whatever it may be.

As a whole, the matrix displays the four situations in which you can find yourself: The M and A market is robust and you must sell, the M and A market is robust and you would like to sell, the M and A market is weak and you must sell, the M and A market is weak and you would like to sell. Each of these situations brings special considerations to your sale decision and requires appropriate responses.

Strong Market / Must Sell or Wish to Sell

Note quadrants 1 and 2 in the matrix. They illustrate the situation in which you must sell or wish to sell, and the market is strong and active. This is an ideal situation, and swift entry could seize the advantage while leaving time for disciplined marketing of your sale.

Weak Market / Wish to Sell

Quadrant 3 highlights when the M and A market is lackluster and you aren't compelled to sell. Here, you have greater flexibility in strategizing and timing a sale. A thorough look at factors critical to the timing decision will help you decide whether to test the market sooner or later. Because business cycles tend to run three to five years, you might consider alternatives within that window.

The first step is to examine your business's current performance and to project performance over the three-year to five-year period. With those results in hand, you can assess what competitors are doing and how the industry may perform, expand, or change during the period. Most important, you need to determine if any of your competitive advantages will be sustained during the cycle, or if there is risk they will erode, making the company less attractive as a candidate for sale. Once you understand these factors, you along with your advisors will be able to determine when you should enter the market.

Weak Market / Must Sell

The environment represented by Quadrant 4 is the most challenging. The selling environment is weak, yet you are motivated, perhaps compelled, to sell. This situation requires thorough due diligence and weighing every means to achieve sale.

Due diligence in a Weak Market / Must Sell situation has a single-minded purpose: find your most forceful sales propositions.

- Is your company outperforming its competitors and its sector? A star business is most likely to attract a buyer.
- Does your company have unique superiorities? Any advantage—better technology, attractive market footprints, highly developed Internet sales platforms—may make your company attractive and saleable even in slow markets.
- Are earnings in your company's sector more robust than the economy generally? If so, you can position your company as a countercyclical prospect.
- Deals of what magnitudes are still being done? A company valued under $50 million may draw buyers when larger deals are nonexistent.
- Is your industry consolidating? Acquiring your company may elevate a local operation into a regional or national power.
- Are foreign buyers hunting for acquisitions? U.S. buyers are not the only prospective buyers.

Alternatives During Weak Markets

As anyone who's been in business knows, times sometimes just plain aren't good. Occasionally, it's true for the economy overall, and sometimes it's true for a particular industry or a company in an unfortunate locale. In fact, some industries and geographies seem to be locked in permanent desperation when customers aren't buying products and neither strategic nor financial buyers are buying companies. Weak M and A markets demand innovative thinking to make sale of your business a reality. Several strategies have proven useful and appealing to sellers and buyers.

Employee Stock Ownership Plan Sale

When M and A markets aren't receptive to your best sale efforts, one alternative for a Chapter C corporation with strong earnings and capable management is selling your company's stock to an Employee Stock Ownership Plan (ESOP).

We discussed ESOPs in chapter 8 and noted what they essentially are— namely, a means for employees to own stock in the company they work for. There, we discussed their tax benefits and usefulness in situations where several owners have different agenda for selling a company. Here, however, we consider ESOPs as a potential buyer of your company when other desirable buyers don't appear.

To begin with, if your company has the right financial profile, you can create an ESOP at any time and in any market. You are in control of the timing. There is tremendous flexibility in designing an ESOP strategy. Your sale to an ESOP can be in a single transaction or structured in two or more transactions. If you would like to cash out some stock now, work for several more years, then fully cash out your remaining stock as you retire, you can arrange to do so. If your company prospers over those years, you will be able to sell your remaining block of stock for a higher value than in the initial transaction. Whether it prospers or not, if your follow-on transaction is a sale of the controlling interest in the company, under the fair market value rules you will get a premium per share because of the control factor. Or if you prefer, at the time you are ready to retire, you can evaluate the M and A market and determine whether it would be more beneficial to sell your remaining stock to the ESOP or to sell your company to a third party.

Although you will only receive a fair market value per share for your sale to an ESOP and not a strategic value, the after-tax results may prove superior to selling to a third party at a low multiple and paying capital gains tax. Remember that if you have a C-corporation you may avail yourself of the Section 1042 rollover option with your proceeds and defer capital gains for a long time or even indefinitely. Not only do you get the use of the full cash value of the sale, but you get the advantage of the investment return on that capital for many years.

In truth, it's not entirely fair to regard ESOPs as a buyer of last resort on an also-ran alternative if other buyers don't appear. Under some circumstances, selling your company to its employees through an ESOP might be your preferred choice.

Seller Financing

Because availability of credit likely will be diminished in weak M and A markets, most buyers prefer or need to include credit in their purchase structure. This is an opportunity for you to seal a transaction by offering creative financing. A buyer may even agree to a higher price if you will finance the transaction. Be sure to have your team do an analysis and forecast of the future results of the company under the control of the new buyer if you consider this option. Include a cash flow analysis to assure that under reasonable expectations of company performance the buyer will be able to service the debt to you comfortably over the term of the promissory note.

Equity Recapitalization

You might consider negotiating an equity recapitalization, selling 70 percent or 80 percent of the company and retaining a minority interest until a specified date or the occurrence of a specified event. Equity recapitalization permits the buyer to acquire control while paying for a part of the company. You benefit with a fair price per share and opportunity for greater returns when your minority interest is liquidated (see figure 9.2).

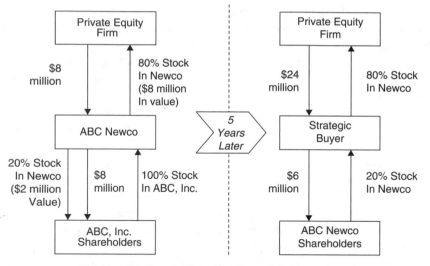

Total to ABC Shareholder: $8 million + $6 million = $14 million

Figure 9.2 Sale and Equity Recap

In this example, ABC, Inc. shareholders sell to a private equity firm for $10 million. At closing, ABC shareholders receive cash of $8 million and the remaining $2 million in the form of the common stock of ABC Newco.

Five years later, the private equity firm is able to triple the value of ABC Newco and has struck a deal with a strategic buyer to sell the company for $30 million. At sale, ABC shareholders (now ABC Newco shareholders) receive $6 million in cash and the private equity firm gets $24 million. As a result, ABC shareholders got $8 000,000 in the first sale to the private equity firm. Then, because they were willing to take a calculated risk and keep a minority share of the surviving company—a risk that paid off handsomely—they received another $6 million at the second sale. Their total cash out equals $14 million.

Earn-outs

A third innovative strategy for selling your business in a weak market is to offer an earn-out. In an earn-out arrangement, the buyer pays you an agreed-upon price—one that, for example, may represent 50 percent to 80 percent of your company's value—at closing. This transaction will usually be negotiated on a fair market value or financial value basis. The buyer then makes further payouts to you, as negotiated, over an agreed period of time. The amount of each scheduled further payment is determined by a formula tied to your company's earnings during that period. The higher the earnings, the higher is the payment to you. This works well when you remain as a manager or contractor with some influence over the company's performance.

Stock-for-Stock Transactions

Stock-for-stock deals are another option in a slow market, as they don't require a buyer to relinquish cash or acquire debt. The strategy works best when selling to a public company. After the legally required restricted period, you can liquidate stock acquired in the transaction. Careful analysis of the public company's strength, solvency, and prospects over the next several years will assure that the trade will be a good one. In any case, you should investigate single-stock management strategies, including hedging opportunities, to see if they would be beneficial in reducing the risk of losing value over your holding period.

Conclusion

In an ideal situation, you'd be a motivated seller in an active M and A market selling to a strategic buyer paying a premium for your company. But just as time and tide wait for no one, the time isn't always right and the tide may be against you. Even then, however, you have alternatives. If you understand your motives for selling and have the persistence to pursue out-of-the-ordinary possibilities, you can position yourself for the best outcome that circumstances permit.

Takeaway Lessons

- Larger M and A markets aren't always congenial to your particular sale or, at times, anybody's sale. However, your sale may be an exception to the prevailing desuetude in broad markets, especially if you're in an industry that's rationalizing, the size of your transaction fits the current market, or your firm is stronger and more attractive than other candidates for purchase. You need to understand what constitutes a strong or weak market, the conditions of the market at your particular time, and whether your firm is an exception to them.
- Nonetheless, you may need to consider alternatives for your sale, including ESOPs, recapitalizations, earn-outs, and stock-for-stock sales. Each of these alternatives potentially can overcome poor M and A markets, and each may offer outcomes that suit your preferences in a transaction. But each is complicated and requires expert guidance.
- Timing isn't solely an issue of markets. It's also a matter of your motivation to sell and, most especially, your urgency in selling. Perhaps you have the good fortune of your motivations and urgency and markets being aligned, and you're in a situation combining a strong market and a wish to sell. This may not be the case for you or the market, however. In such cases, you can follow a decision matrix to help you position yourself for the best, whatever "the best" may be at that moment.

For additional resources and tools, visit www.sellingyourbusinessformore.com

CHAPTER 10

How to Engage the Market: Selecting the Best Process for Selling

Introduction

Everyone wins when you place your business before the right buyers through the right selling process. This chapter discusses approaches to that process plus the appeals and drawbacks of each. Marketing a business for sale is the special province of the team's investment banking firm. Its insights into the business, understanding of your objectives and preferences, and reading of the market will focus you and your team on the best way to begin, execute, and conclude the sale of your business.

Three Approaches to Selling

The three common approaches to selling a business are a broad auction, a limited auction, and a targeted-buyer campaign. Selected situations may require combining these three approaches.

Broad Auction

A broad auction process begins by identifying and contacting an array of potential buyers. You gradually narrow the field as you and your team investigate potential buyers' financial capability, their suitability for your goals in selling, and other pertinent considerations. Finally, you and your sale team spotlight the most promising few.

You then solicit initial offers and initiate negotiations with the best candidates to elicit their top offer. You and your team evaluate each offer for price, deal structure, risks to performance and closing, advantages and disadvantages, and business and material contingencies. You and your buyer reach a deal, sign a contract, and conduct final due diligence until closing, when your business or assets change hands.

Advantages of a Broad Auction
The broad auction has several advantages:

- Starting with a broad universe of potential buyers—foreign, strategic, financial—allows you the broadest exposure to the market.
- You will have greater certainty that the sale represents the highest price and best terms available, because you have explored all other prospects.
- Contacting a wider field of prospective buyers offers you a better chance to attract competing bidders.

Disadvantages of a Broad Auction
Disadvantages include:

- Contacting and performing due diligence on a larger number of prospective buyers take more time and expense.
- Because you've contacted the largest number of potential buyers, word is more likely to leak that your business is for sale.
- You'll spend more time on presentations and question-and-answer sessions with a greater number of semifinalists.

A Limited Auction

A limited auction is a smaller version of a broad auction. Although the number of screened and contacted candidates will be smaller, you will have assured that prospects represent a reasonable cross-section of buyer categories. Numbers at each stage of the process are correspondingly smaller than in a broad auction, but you still have potential for competition among buyers. It offers many advantages of the broader auction but transpires over a shorter time with less expense.

Generally, a limited auction best serves businesses that are a single entity in a single location. A unique enterprise, such as an internationally recognized brand name luxury retailer, may do best with a full global auction. A company or asset that's a strategic fit with only a handful of buyers will do best with a targeted process.

Advantages of a Limited Auction
Such a limited auction has several advantages:

- There is a considerable cost savings in working through a process with a smaller number of candidates. Fewer information memorandum books have to be produced; there is less legal review with fewer confidentiality agreements, letters of intent, proposed PSA's.
- The elapsed time from launching the marketing to closing the deal is typically shorter than that of a full blown auction.

- Some buyers refuse to participate in a very large auction but will engage in a limited auction process.

Disadvantages of a Limited Auction
But there are disadvantages as well:

- You are very dependent on the strength of your advisors' insights on how to define the target candidates.
- You will never know if you have missed an opportunity by limiting exposure.

A Targeted-Buyer Campaign

This approach is highly selective at the outset. An investment banker will apply highly distilled criteria to identify only the most likely qualified buyers. Examples might include a strategic buyer known to be seeking an acquisition like your company, a strategic buyer or large competitor attracted by obvious synergies, or a competitor who's previously shown interest in a purchase.

The targeted-buyer approach resembles an auction in that confidentiality agreements are signed before identifying information is shared. There is usually much more interaction and contact by investment bankers.

Advantages of Targeted-Buyer Campaigns
A targeted-buyer approach has several advantages:

- You perform more due diligence on buyer candidates initially; therefore, those who survive vetting tend to be interested, capable, and reliable.
- The process usually takes less time, and negotiations begin sooner.
- This approach lends itself to a confidential sale because fewer people are involved and interaction among parties can be tightly controlled.

Disadvantage of Targeted-Buyer Campaigns
The disadvantage of a targeted-buyer approach is that over-rigorous selection criteria may exclude potential buyers from consideration. For example, a prospect may escape notice because it was an uncharacteristic buyer—say, a smaller company seeking to acquire a larger company.

Combination of Approaches

You might consider a combination of approaches if you're not selling your entire company in a stock sale but you are selling two or more holdings separately.

For example, XYZ Company owns a manufacturing business that produces bearings through a highly proprietary, unique, and efficient process. ABC also owns twenty acres of land near an interstate highway interchange, making the location suitable for industrial and warehouse development. The manufacturing business would appeal to domestic and global manufacturers who benefit from acquiring a proprietary process, but these manufacturers may have no interest in the land. The land will, however, appeal to real estate developers or industrial builders.

A few buyers may be interested in acquiring XYZ as a whole, but it's more likely XYZ could sell the bearing company and the land separately. Therefore, XYZ may opt to sell the bearing business through a broad or limited auction while conducting a targeted-buyer campaign to sell the land.

Overview of the Sale Process

Each approach toward marketing your business is slightly different in its activities and its usefulness in each situation. But regardless of which approach you choose, the total process of selling your business includes a set of common components and embodies a set of common actions.

Selecting the Right Approach

The investment banker and your selling team will identify potential buyers and decide which sales approach is appropriate. This is your chance to express your objectives for selling the business—your continued employment under the buyer, for instance, or your wish to retain certain managers and guarantee employee benefits after the deal. If your company has a culture of supporting community endeavors, perhaps you'll insist on a buyer with the same culture. Perhaps you prefer selling to a buyer in your industry instead of financial buyers, feeling they aren't long-term operators committed to a business. Air any predilections important to you at this point.

Discussions with an investment banker must include your financial risk preferences and tolerance. Decide if you want to cash out entirely upon selling or will entertain a deal with cash and follow-on payments, an equity recapitalization, an earn-out, or even seller financing. If you're selling assets separately, investigate both selling assets and selling your firm's stock. You'll want to decide, first, whether one strategy is preferable from a selling perspective—that is, whether there are enough interested buyers. Second, you'll estimate what after-tax receipts are likely with a single deal compared to multiple deals.

Your investment banker will have a recommendation concerning likely types of buyers for your firm or separate assets and which sales approach may yield the best outcome. With estimates of your firm's value from an independent evaluator and your investment banker's projections, your accountant can model a range of after-tax return for sale of the whole or part of the company. As owner, you evaluate the information and recommendations and weigh the chance for larger returns from multiple deals against the hassle and risk of negotiating and closing with several buyers.

By knowing your preferences and the weight you place on them plus your firm's characteristics and its industry, investment bankers should be able to recommend buyers to be approached and the sale process to be chosen. Listen to your experts when selecting the sales approach. They have done the legwork and will recommend approaches tailored for your transaction.

Once you and your team have thought through these matters carefully, the actual selling of your firm begins.

Contacting Prospective Buyers

You, your investment banker, and your selling team will agree on the universe of likely buyers. Your initial contact with them features only generic information about your company to test their level of interest. You might contact the most likely buyers personally, whereas you might send others an e-mail teaser. During initial contact, you will never include information that makes your company immediately identifiable.

Interested parties will respond to your investment banker, who sends each one a confidentiality agreement to sign before continuing. Like many owners, you probably prefer not to broadcast that your company is for sale. Intimation of an impending sale disrupts employees and may disconcert vendors and customers. Hearing your business is on the block, competitors may leverage market advantage by disparaging the ongoing viability of your operation. The confidentiality agreement forbids potential buyers from disclosing the fact of the sale or information gleaned during their due diligence.

Developing Interest

At the next stage of the selling process, your investment banker presents prospective buyers a fundamental description of your company and its financial statements. As your investment banker evaluates buyers, their financial capabilities, and the seriousness of their interest, it will present a formal information memorandum to those who pass muster. During this time, the investment banker presents each potential buyer its persuasive arguments for why your firm is an attractive acquisition. It doubtless tailors versions of this presentation to match the inclinations of each prospective buyer.

Having met prospective buyers and tested their earnestness, the investment banker will recommend a range of sales prices for your firm. It also will suggest a threshold price for consideration in any further expression of interest. It's unusual to set an asking price. Your intention is to generate competing bids, and setting an asking price defeats that intention.

As the field of interested buyers narrows, the most qualified and serious buyers may seek access to elements of your due diligence. To entice buyers further, you and your team might join the investment banker's presentations, making more persuasive use of your knowledge about the business, its market, and its prospects. If no presentations are scheduled, managers should be available to answer the more intricate questions about your firm and their responsibilities. As this is progressing, your team and the investment banker cull the likely buyers to find the most likely buyer.

Commencing the Close

Your investment banker will set a date for serious and qualified buyers to submit a letter of intent. The letter sets out the price and terms they're willing to offer for your business. Instead of a letter of intent, the investment banker may suggest circulating a proposed form of purchase and sale contract, asking buyers to complete it with their offering prices and terms. This is generally used when sales terms are complicated by the nature of a particular business. Although each buyer will suggest modifications, contracts will be generally comparable. Thus, it will be an easier exercise for the team to identify the best offer and buyer.

Evaluating Offers

Once the letters or contracts submitted, the investment banker and your team evaluate offers. Price is certainly important, but terms, contingencies, and escrows have considerable bearing on prioritizing buyers. Likelihood of closing the deal and time required to do so are two highly significant considerations. A longer closing period leaves you more vulnerable to market downturns, earnings interruptions, financing difficulties, and every other deal-killing risk. Buyers with strong financial positions and proposed capital structures with already approved debt are preferable to buyers still assembling their consortium of backers. And, of course, some offers will or won't align with priorities and values you've established for the transaction.

Together, you and your team select a favored few offers. Negotiating then begins in earnest. The investment banker will have insights into negotiating strategies likely to be effective with each remaining contender, but you and your advisors have a voice in that determination. If you have a clear preference for one buyer or dislike of another, make it known. As negotiations progress, investment bankers try to gin up competition among buyers. If they're successful, you'll have leverage and latitude to extract a buyer's top price and most favorable terms. All that remain are to choose the best deal and settle contract terms.

Conclusion

The selling process you select will depend on your intention to sell all or part of your business, the type of business you have, and the preferences of sellers. Financial markets are flexible and innovative in creating possibilities for your successful sale, but, at times, markets will be more receptive to one sale approach over another. The actual sale of your business—the number of potential buyers contacted, the acceptance of bids, negotiations—will unfold in line with the process you initially selected. And, as always, when you engage the market, the right forethought and the right team are as important as the right process.

Takeaway Lessons

- Selling your business is a process, and it's essential to pick the right approach for the type of business, the nature of assets you're selling, and characteristics of likely buyers. Each of those considerations, along with your needs and goals, will determine whether you choose a broad auction, limited auction, targeted-buyer campaign, or a combination of these.
- Even though each of the three approaches differs, each will unfold in similar ways. After selecting your approach, you will progress through contacting buyers, developing interest among them, evaluating offers, negotiating, and closing. As always, competent counsel is indispensable.
- Whichever approach you select, everything we've discussed so far will apply to it—your personal values, motivation and urgency, inclination for a type of buyer, preference to remain with your firm or to depart, your desired outcome, and your vision for your life and your business's future after the sale.

For additional resources and tools, visit www.sellingyourbusinessformore.com

CHAPTER 11

Preparing the Paperwork:
Documents Attendant to Your Sale

Introduction

It's essential to understand every document pertaining to the sale of your business. Otherwise, you may be saddled with a legion of legal and financial problems and a legacy of future worry. Most documents relating to your sale result from a negotiation of some type. You might think that agreeing upon a sales price is the only—or at least most significant—negotiation that takes place. In fact, everything involved in selling your business is a negotiation, and every negotiation produces paperwork.

You will quickly discover that contracts and agreements aren't the only paperwork you'll face. Depending on the size and complexity of your sale, you and your team may be assembling almost every document your company has produced, starting with its articles of incorporation and ending with yesterday's employee newsletter. Controlling and safeguarding this information is essential to orderly diligence.

Some sale negotiations proceed briskly to a conclusion; others are interrupted by delays for external approvals or through a buyer's intractability on language addressing significant issues. Finally, your deal will need to be structured with purchase terms that work for you and your buyer.

Documents Attendant to Your Sale

Let's begin by looking at the range of documents that pertain to negotiations and due diligence. Although not all might apply to your particular sale, most will. They follow a prescribed sequence and have specific purposes in advancing your deal. Understanding them is essential, just as it's essential to understand pitfalls you'll want to avoid and stipulations you'll want to include.

Confidentiality Agreement

The first significant document of your sale process is the *confidentiality agreement*. When you're searching for advisors—for instance, valuation experts or investment bankers—or when you are providing information to prospective buyers, you must protect your business's confidential and proprietary information. It is not unheard of for a business to pose as a prospective buyer to gain access to information about competitors. Financial reports and environmental reports can exhibit a company's strengths and weaknesses. Knowing your weaknesses, in particular, can help a competitor devote resources to gain market share.

Nonetheless, you must provide detailed information about your company and its operations to prospective buyers so they can conduct their own due diligence. Likewise, investment bankers need to know details of your company's financial structure, ownership, financial performance, and plans to construct their proposal for positioning and marketing your company.

The confidentiality agreement, commonly called a "Confi" (pronounced con'fee), often requires that all information provided:

- Will be treated as confidential if it is not generally available to the public
- Will not be disclosed to others
- Will be shared with employees, advisors, or representatives only to the extent necessary to construct a proposal
- Will be destroyed if the proposal is not accepted

The confidentiality agreement will set out penalties for breaching any of its terms and may include other provisions, depending on circumstances particular to your company and your sale.

Your confidentiality agreement should be drafted by your corporate counsel or external transaction counsel you've hired. It must be available early enough in the process that you can provide it to prospective valuation firms or investment banks before you request proposals for their services. When you begin to speak with buyers, expect that they will want to modify the agreement. Drafting counsel in collaboration with your team will determine which provisions are indispensable and which are open to change. Everyone usually is able to compromise on mutually acceptable language, but some potential buyers are so adamant about provisions unacceptable to sellers that no agreement can be reached. Although these instances are frustrating, it's better to weed out such an obstinate prospective buyer early.

Sales Memorandum (Confidential Information Memorandum)

When the confidentiality agreement is completed, you've provided relevant information, and chosen an investment banker, the investment banker will construct a *sales memorandum*, also known as a *confidential information memorandum*.

The sales memorandum is a marketing piece intended to entice prospective buyers with basic information about your company.

Your investment banker will suggest a sales plan for your company. After initially qualifying prospective buyers and receiving signed confidentiality agreements, this intermediary's first substantive contact with the prospective buyers will be to provide the sales memorandum. The investment banker constructs the sales memorandum from information you provide and from its knowledge and research into your industry and market. Your company accountant and operating managers may be asked to contribute detail that makes your company most appealing to prospective buyers.

The sales memorandum will often include the following information, illustrated with colorful photographs and charts:

- Executive summary that describes your company and what exactly is being sold
- Key features of the company:
  — Uniqueness of the company, its products, and services
  — Scarcity of what the company has to offer
  — Flexibility of zoning, convenience of access, and range of possible uses for company property
  — Level of profitability
  — Market segment
- History of your company and details of capital reinvestment and management structure
- Industry and market overview and trends
- Financial overview

Letter of Intent

A *letter of intent* (LOI) is a preliminary agreement between you and a prospective buyer that sets out understandings between parties about to begin contract negotiations. The LOI provides a framework for negotiations and identifies specific issues of the transaction before spending extensive time and money on multiple drafts of contracts. It also facilitates in meeting a board of director's requirements and regulatory requirements while negotiations progress.

Although the LOI often states price and terms of the sale, they usually are nonbinding. Some LOIs do contain binding provisions, such as terms establishing an exclusivity period for the potential buyer and permitting that candidate access to your business, its managers, and the due diligence room. This document can be prepared by your transaction attorney or the buyer's, but it is always negotiated with the other party. Before you agree to a LOI, be certain all material terms of the deal—price, structure, post-closing terms, and contingencies—are clear. Binding and nonbinding terms should be labeled as such.

You should be aware of the disadvantages inherent in LOIs.

- Extended negotiation of the terms of the LOI may delay drafting and negotiation of the purchase/sale agreement.
- Drafting and negotiating two agreements will require considerably more time and cost than going directly to a purchase/sale agreement.
- Although the LOI specifies that price and terms of sale and other provisions are nonbinding, courts may find ambiguity and rule otherwise.
- Your leverage is greatest before the LOI (or Purchase and Sale Agreement, if there is no LOI) is signed; therefore, you relinquish some negotiating power.
- Signing a LOI in haste means your team may not have time to think through practical business issues associated with the sale.
- A buyer's greatest incentive for signing a LOI is to obtain exclusivity and if possible to lock in favorable terms and avoid an auction environment. You benefit most from competing bidders.

Purchase/Sale Agreement

A properly constructed *purchase/sale agreement* (PSA) is as important as the selling price. As you negotiate the sale price, you should be negotiating terms of the PSA, for it can have a material financial impact on all parties. Capable transaction counsel is essential to drafting a PSA that will not continue to cost you money after closing the sale. Your legal counsel can draft a PSA favorable to you and offer it to a qualified buyer as a starting document.

A typical PSA will include the following provisions:

- Names of the seller and buyer
- Structure of the transaction, whether a merger, stock sale, or asset sale
- What is being sold—for instance, your firm's stock or specific assets
- Liabilities to be assumed
- Sale price
- Deposit
- Payment—for instance cash, debt and what collateral secures it, or stock from a purchasing company
- Date of closing
- Sellers' representations and warranties (discussed in detail later in this section)
- Buyers' representation and warranties
- Covenant not to compete (discussed in detail later in this section)
- Conditions to closing
- Breakup fee
- Dispute resolution
- Governing law

- Notices
- Signature block

Representations and Warranties

Although the entire PSA is important and should be constructed carefully, one of its most contentious sections is *representations and warranties*. A *representation* is a statement about past or existing facts. A *warranty* is a promise or guarantee pertaining to existing or future facts. Representations and warranties are usually dealt with together in one section of the PSA.

If you represent and/or warrant that certain information is true, it ought to be true. Misstatements can cost you significantly even if they are inadvertent and without malicious intent. For example, in disclosure documents you might have forgotten a long-dormant "slip and fall" legal action, or you might mistakenly have believed a retroactive union negotiation was settled. If you are unsure, you should qualify your statement as being "to the best of the seller's knowledge."

The smaller and more straightforward the business being sold, the less the need for representations and warranties. The need will be greater if your business is larger, its operations more complicated, and its products more technical. Representations and warranties verify such matters as:

- You or your business are a duly organized corporation.
- You have the requisite authority to enter into the agreement.
- Financial statements are true and complete in all material respects.
- You have disclosed all liabilities.
- You have a good and marketable fee simple interest in real estate included in the sale.
- You have disclosed all outstanding or pending litigations involving your company or its assets.
- All current labor agreements are disclosed.
- Copies of employee benefit plans are true and complete.

Representations and warranties refer to disclosure schedules that provide details in each appropriate category. These disclosure schedules must be accurate and complete to assure you are protected under terms of the document.

The buyer will seek every opportunity possible for you to reimburse him. You can minimize the potential financial impact of representations and warranties by limiting the time period during which claims can be brought and by limiting the amount of reimbursable claims. For example, you might propose that claims be filed within a reasonable time, such as eighteen months. Further, you can propose that total claims be limited by a threshold and a cap. To avoid aggregating large numbers of nonmaterial claims that would reach the threshold for indemnification, you can attach a materiality requirement for each claim counted for that purpose.

Your success in negotiating the claim period, threshold, and cap will depend on the buyer's intractability and how many suitors your firm attracts. Similarly, your ability to negotiate favorable representations and warranties will depend on how earnestly a prospective buyer wants your company and the level of competition he senses for its purchase. Your transaction attorney and investment banker will offer insights into the range and structure of representations and warranties, indemnification provisions, escrows, and claims periods that pertained in similar transactions. Their expertise can provide negotiating leverage.

Covenant Not to Compete

Fearing that you or a manager in your business might start a rival firm or join a competitor, buyers customarily want to limit your ability to compete against them in the future. Therefore, they will insert into the PSA a *covenant not to compete*. Also called a *noncompetition clause*, it restricts your ability to engage in rival business activities within a specified geography or time.

As with nearly all items in the PSA, a covenant not to compete is negotiated. You will want the restricted business activity to be defined precisely. For instance, the buyer of your software firm might prefer you not be in the software business at all for two years. You might respond with an offer not to enter a market niche, such as accounting software systems, or that it should take the buyer only one year to establish itself with the customer base.

You should be compensated for restricting your right to do business any time and anywhere. Note, however, that tax treatment for such compensation might differ from taxation on proceeds from selling your business.

A typical covenant not to compete will contain:

- Names of the parties involved
- Amount of payment you receive for agreeing to the covenant
- Description of the restricted activity
- Delineation of the geographical area in which the restriction applies
- Description of the time period applicable to the limitation of activity
- Acknowledgment of action the buyer will take if you breach the covenant

Due Diligence Room

As you see, prospective buyers and their financers will be eager for detailed information about your company, much of it highly sensitive. Therefore, it's common practice to establish a *due diligence room* where they can examine needed information while assuring it remains under your control and out of public view.

The due diligence room can be a physical location or a virtual site offering Internet access via password to data accessible digitally. Your investment banker and transaction counsel will prepare a schedule of its necessary documents.

Your accountant, corporate attorney or general counsel, and internal managers usually assemble much of the requested material. If you provide a virtual room, your advisors will suggest services that can scan and sort materials. Serious buyers will need and demand extensive detail about your company, and laying needed information in a well constructed due diligence room will prevent headaches later.

Not all prospective buyers are equal in their interest in your firm or their ability to consummate a deal. It may be wise to make only part of the due diligence room's information available to buyers who may be "bottom feeding" or are unlikely to find financing.

The quantity and variety of information in your due diligence room will vary according to the size of your company and the complexity of your business and industry. When a great deal of information is required, a virtual due diligence room may offer a number of advantages over a physical location. A virtual room can provide information via the Internet, eliminating need to find a physical location and to supervise prospective buyers while in the room.

In fact, it is often wise not to have the due diligence room on your premises. The presence of the room and the traffic of prospective buyers may alert employees and make it difficult to keep sale of your company confidential. Your investment banker and other counsel advising on the sale will know about virtual due diligence rooms and firms that provide those services.

A typical due diligence room may contain:

- General corporate materials and all basic information about your company
  — Organizational chart
  — List of subsidiaries
  — List of shareholders
  — Sales memorandum
  — Corporate books, which will include articles of incorporation, bylaws, and minutes of board meetings
- Contracts
  — List of vendors
  — Contracts, which might include rental, maintenance and software licensing agreements
- Licenses and permits
  — List of and copies of licenses, which might include licenses to engage in certain lines of business such as restaurants and bars
  — List of and copies of permits, which might include permits to build and operate elevators, a boiler, or industrial size air conditioners
- Litigation
  — List of outstanding litigation, which might include litigation with clients, vendors, or current and former employees
  — List of litigation attorneys used and copies of audit letters from those attorneys listing outstanding litigation

- Noncompliance with regulations
  — List current complaints from OSHA and local regulators. If none exists, say so.
  — List current actions under way to correct noncompliance. Noncompliance can be associated with matters such as fire prevention, environmental complaints, and emergency action plans
- Employee matters
  — Life insurance policies
  — Benefits plans
  — Employee handbook
  — Job descriptions
  — Collective bargaining agreements
- Information systems
  — List of software used for any purpose, including financial systems
  — List of hardware, including computers and printers
  — Copy of the Information Technology Disaster Recovery Plan
- Intellectual property
  — List of brands and trademarks
  — List of licenses to perform certain services or activities
- Environmental
  — Copies of all environment reports
  — List of EPA certifications, such as periodic groundwater testing
- Real property
  — List of parcels
  — Title reports
  — Leases and easements
  — Surveys and property drawings
- Other property
  — Schedule of vehicles and any other equipment
  — List of artwork or any other property
- Financial documents
  — Several years of internal financial statements
  — Recent quarterly financial statements
  — Several years of audit reports
  — Depreciation lapsing schedules
  — Real property tax invoices
  — Pertinent detailed expenses—for example, operating or headquarters expenses
  — Financial forecasts
  — Several years of tax returns
  — Uniform Commercial Code searches
- Copies of all insurance policies, including general liability, umbrella, auto, and terrorism risk

- Customer information, including demographic data about your customer base
- Sale agreement form

Immediate Closing and Delayed Closing

Some transactions are simple and can be executed when a contract is signed. For example, a minority shareholder may agree to sell ten shares to another shareholder for cash. However, most sales of businesses or of substantially all its assets require an interval between the date the contract is signed and when the transaction actually closes. The delay may be necessary because other shareholders must approve the deal, the buyer needs more time to finalize due diligence and lock in financing, or regulatory approvals are needed.

The contract will describe what you and the buyer must do to resolve issues that caused the delay and to assure you maintain the status quo between signing the contract and closing. It may also stipulate material events whose occurrence allows either party to walk away from the deal. For the buyer, these may be acts of God, such a hurricane destroying the plant or an irreparable downturn in business; for the seller, failure of the buyer to acquire a necessary license.

Common reasons for delayed closing include the need to obtain regulatory or shareholder approvals and the existence of covenants involving third parties.

Regulatory Approvals

Currently, in any transaction where the purchase price exceeds $15 million or in which any person or corporate entity will acquire more than 15 percent of a company's voting stock, your counsel should clarify whether a Hart-Scott-Rodino (HSR) notification is required. This obligation arises from federal antitrust laws that mandate the Federal Trade Commission to be notified of possible antitrust issues. If an HSR is required, you may not complete the sale until a required waiting period has expired or further action is expected from Federal Trade Commission or Department of Justice.

Another example is Federal Communications Commission approval of licenses involving radio, television, or wireless communications firms. The contract needs to indicate if industry sector regulatory approvals are required and specify whether the buyer or the seller is to seek the approval.

Shareholder Approval

Most states require an affirmative vote of a majority of shareholders to consummate a transaction involving a substantial sale of a company's assets or the company itself. Bylaws of the corporation or the operating agreement of a partnership or limited liability corporation may specify that a supermajority of equity holders must affirm a material transaction of this type.

Third Party Approvals

Debt covenants may require permission from the lender to transfer owner-ship. Contracts with customers or vendors also may require their consent in order to be transferable to a buyer. As part of contract negotiations, you may agree to make reasonable efforts to transfer these contracts, and the buyer may assume responsibility to negotiate with parties whom your efforts haven't satisfied.

Structural Issues

Sale of your business needs to be structured in a number of ways, but the most important is the type of payment agreed on for purchasing your business or part of its assets.

Share Purchase

The simplest type of transaction is a share purchase in which the new owner merely buys your firm's stock. Because the purchased business remains unchanged, individual assets and liabilities need not be separately transferred, although change of control provisions might apply to outside contracts or to arrangements with employees. These need to be understood and fulfilled.

If you sell your firm's stock for cash, that is articulated in the purchase agreement. If you exchange your stock for stock in the buyer's firm—or mostly stock with some cash—the transaction may qualify as a tax free exchange. In this latter case, restrictions on your right to resale the buyer's stock also will be specified. If the buyer is a publicly traded company, terms in the transac-tion will specify conditions under which you may sell the stock after a holding period expires.

Asset Purchase

If the sale of your company is structured as an asset purchase, the buyer acquires some or all of its assets and usually also the named liabilities associated with them. Which assets are acquired and what liabilities the buyer assumes are, again, negotiated. Asset purchase deals tend to be complex, deeply involving your transaction counsel and investment banker in negotiating details and doc-umenting them accurately in the PSA.

Merger

Following a merger, either your company or the buyer's company ceases to exist. If the buyer's, the contract is simpler because your prior agreements and arrangements remain in force (except for situations involving change of control agreements). If your company ceases to exist, all issues pertaining to an asset purchase arise.

Conclusion

You have to negotiate almost every aspect of the sale of your business and sign many documents to effectuate its sale. Although you will rely on experienced counsel and advisors to help you, do not abdicate your responsibilities in understanding and reviewing the paperwork. To outsource this too far could create problems in the short- and long term. The selling price is just one of many crucial elements of the sale. It's essential that you consult your transaction advisors and counsel to assure you understand the details and responsibilities in those legal documents and, to the extent possible, assure their provisions are favorable to you.

Legal documents are just part of a larger collection of the paperwork you and your team will have to assemble. You will have to go back in time to your articles of incorporation and, from there, through to the latest client, supplier, or employee communication. Keeping this archive orderly, current, and secure is important to the sales process.

Takeaway Lessons

- Whoever said "Talk is easy" never had to document selling a business. Everything you intend to tell a prospective buyer needs to be documented in due diligence and confidentiality agreements. Everything you preliminarily agree to needs to be documented in letters of intent, and everything you are about to agree to belongs in purchase/sale agreements. What you actually agree to must be documented in contracts and provisions of other documents, such as noncompete clauses. You even have to document approvals from people you might never talk to—regulators, for example.
- Extensive documentation needs extensive review and tight control. Therefore, again, competent counsel is essential, as are mechanisms such as due diligence rooms, which restrict disseminating sensitive business material to only the appropriate eyes.
- Everything in your sale is a negotiation. No matter how willingly and congenially those negotiations proceed, you will nonetheless pay profound attention to matters that short-circuit your business future (such as highly constraining noncompete clauses) or leave you with unpleasant surprise obligations (representations and warranties) after the sale. As Shakespeare wrote, "The evil that men do lives after them; the good is oft' interred with their bones."
- Negotiations don't have to be contentious for there to be delays in your sale. Again, as always, look ahead. Before you become deeply involved in the time

and expense of selling—and before your negotiations might reach sticking points—determine if you need to obtain regulatory approvals, third-party consents, and agreement shareholders or trustees for the deal to go through.

For additional resources and tools, visit www.sellingyourbusinessformore.com

CHAPTER 12

Greater Than the Sum of the Parts: Managing an Integration

Introduction

For a number of reasons—to gain competitive advantage, achieve operational efficiencies, improve market position, diversify risk—you may decide to sell your company to another, larger, enterprise in a merger transaction. If so, you'll likely seek strategic buyers from your industry, because they often can afford to pay more than a financial buyer, given potential synergies and available cost reductions. As we mentioned earlier, we have worked with many firms that launched their selling effort with a specific strategic buyer in mind.

Although they are desirable buyers, a merger, especially with a larger company, is a process completely different from simply transferring ownership of a business from one person to another. A successful *sale* ends when the sale concludes and you're paid for your business. But a successful *sale and merger* requires integrating your organization into another after the sale. And your role in the process may be different if you and the buyer agree to your continued involvement with the new enterprise.

For your sale and merger to be the most attractive to buyers, you should start to think about how to integrate your business at the first moment you think about selling it, whether you are there to make it happen or not. An attitude of "that's not my problem" can actually lessen the value of your business to potential buyers. The goal of a successful integration should guide your deliberations and actions at each stage of the selling process.

Integrating two businesses can be swift and simple if the intent of the merger is to keep both firms relatively separate. Integration is more sophisticated than linking companies legally and changing Web sites. In more complex scenarios, it requires combining business ecosystems, engaging a larger universe of stakeholders, establishing new norms, and growing the merged organization. Integrating two firms after a sale and merger may require change within every function of both organizations and will definitely involve a blending of two, sometimes entirely dissimilar, organizational cultures.

If firms are integrated properly, customers, partners, and employees stay engaged, sales move forward, and productivity does not suffer. Unfortunately, however, a majority of mergers never meet management's strategic and financial expectations. To avoid that common fate, integrating your business after a sale requires clear and realistic goals, focused leadership, and superb execution. You and the new owner will need to design your ongoing role and work in concert as you both deem appropriate. The remainder of this chapter assumes that you do stay involved. Even if yours is a limited involvement, the following discussion will let you know what to expect during the merger process.

Overview of the Integration Process

Ideally, the process of integrating two businesses should begin when you decide to sell to and merge with another firm. You will have a motivation for selling your business, a degree of urgency in doing so, and a goal in mind while engaged in the activities of selling. It will influence many decisions that you make during the process. Therefore, at the start of the selling process, it's reasonable for you to think about integrating your business after it's joined with another.

Integration starts with forming the right strategy to achieve your goals for the sale and acquisition, and it includes identifying potential acquirers and conducting due diligence. In the case of a thorough integration, it continues by assembling the numerous elements of two organizations—their staffs, customers, partners, distribution channels, technologies, products and services, production facilities, and various functional areas. As is the case in managing the business, managing the integration requires oversight, assignment of responsibilities, staff to execute those responsibilities, a goal that marks completion, and a timeline.

Others may argue with us, but it has been our experience that a "merger of equals" really does not exist, no matter what anyone says or truly believes. One of the firms will end up being in control of the other, including during the merger process. If you are being acquired, you bring valuable knowledge of the acquired firm and can work closely with the buyer to design the merger process. If you believe your involvement is important, negotiate this up front. Otherwise the buyer will determine your role.

Although the larger company usually is the dominant one, we have had experiences where the opposite is true. In one example, a much larger firm in a commoditized end of the IT staffing business bought a smaller, niche player with stronger methodology, project work, client relationships, and profits. The larger firm changed its name, methodologies, and offerings to the smaller one's and made additional acquisitions to gain entry into specific geographies, products, and services offerings.

Business integration planning has five stages, each with specific and essential purposes, ranging from the simple case of two companies simply linking and otherwise leaving each other alone to a deep integration across all functional areas.

Stage One: Acquisition Strategies and Implications for Integration

You should start by assessing the merits of your business being acquired. Factors in that decision include benefits from selling to the acquiring company, what is actually being sold, who the logical buyers are, and the type of operational autonomy you seek. View everything through the lens of an acquirer: what and who would find integrating with your firm valuable and why? These decisions also determine the extent and activities of your integration effort. Or, in short, your initial acquisition strategy determines your initial integration strategy. Are you looking to have your business remain fairly independent, or do you think the business and you would be best served with the deep integration scenario? Let's begin with the simple case.

The Simple Case

At the near end of the spectrum of possibilities, integration might mean simply creating a new legal entity. If the acquisition will preserve independence of your business and the acquirer's, less integration is required than when companies are combined in a significant way. If the goal is to keep your business as a stand-alone entity, only connecting and communication points need to be established. As the original owner, you frequently will remain as leader of your business as a unit within the larger organization. Establishing strategic linkages, positioning, communication channels, and governance structures then follows.

Given that your firms will remain relatively independent, it may seem unnecessary to combine your two operating cultures. In fact, it's highly important for two reasons. First, you, as a new member in a larger organization, may need training and an attitude adjustment to work within an organization instead of as its top leader. Second, that also may be true for your employees. They may—appropriately or not, depending on the new unit's degree of autonomy—continue deferring only to you as their formerly independent business owner. You and your employees will need to understand their role in the larger entity and how to succeed within it. It is very important that you and the buyer agree clearly on how your relationship will work and how to communicate it.

Complex Case

At the far end of the spectrum, however, a sale and merger could require sweeping integration of departments, employees, and capital assets. More comprehensively absorbing your acquired business into the combined organization takes more complete integration of processes, people, and cultures. For example, if the expected benefits from your acquisition are interdependence and leveraging both organizations symbiotically, its integration is necessarily more complex.

Company cultures must be understood and the marriage planned carefully. As Thomas Armstrong from *Multiple Intelligences Around the World* put it, "Cultures are like chemical elements. You can mix two of them, and you might get something useful like water or table salt. But you might also blow up the kitchen." You and your management can be critical thinkers in this situation. You know the most about your business, and, therefore, know how to spot opportunities and exploit synergies in this new situation.

If the intent of the merger is to consolidate organizations to eliminate redundancies, streamline operations, and reduce costs, you and your management can be integral to the business integration strategy. It's important in this situation, as in all others, that you remain unbiased during analysis and consolidation. You may tend to judge your business processes and functions, for example, as superior and push for them to become the standard of the combined organization. In this situation, consider appointing an independent and trusted third-party advisor to assist in the evaluation.

Whatever the degree of integration, putting together the communication plan to ensure everyone is operating from the same playbook, as discussed in an earlier chapter and reviewed again in this chapter, is crucial.

Integration and Due Diligence

Whatever the acquisition strategy, your business integration plan and due diligence materials should document the acquisition's ultimate objectives and benefits—for example, reducing expenses and increasing market share or revenue. Document your merger's objectives and benefits early, because later you'll translate them into implementation goals, such as capturing corporate efficiencies and retaining key personnel. As your planning for the integration continues, you'll use integration goals to form project plans to achieve them.

Remember, the majority of mergers do not meet expectations. This is frequently because of ambiguous goals and culture clashes. How will you make sure yours will be a success? Bring in experts where appropriate, document your goals, put concrete action plans around them, hold people accountable, measure results, and always pay attention to your people.

Stage Two: Integration and the Right Acquirer

Once you've decided your strategy and objectives for a merger, you will evaluate potential acquirers based upon those decisions. Preferably, you will identify more than one potential acquirer. It's said that having only one interested buyer is like having none: you have no options or comparisons if you entertain a single buyer, and you likely won't get the best deal for your business or for your employees. However—and it is an important "however"—seeking more than one potential buyer means you may need to consider more than one integration strategy at the outset.

At this stage, too, you should realize that the questions you deliberate concerning choice of a buyer will be the questions that launch your ensuing integration strategy.

- What is my reason for considering this merger?
- Will my business remain an independent company with me in charge, or will it be integrated into the buying organization?
- What are the advantages of selling to a particular buyer?
- What synergies and benefits do I expect, and how can they be quantified and measured?
- What must I do to realize them?
- Do I feel strongly about what happens to the employees, customers, suppliers, and community as a result of the merger? If so, how should that impact the effort?
- What do I want my role to be in the integration effort? Do I want to hand over the reigns quickly or shepherd the effort over time?

And then the critical question: How will my integration plan assure those objectives are met efficiently in the established time frame?

Broad Definition of Due Diligence

Preparing for integration while seeking a buyer takes a broader than usual definition of due diligence. Most companies regard due diligence as the means for evaluating financial, operational, and managerial capabilities and strength. They concentrate on financial viability, product and service compatibility, value of the merger, and closing the deal. But they frequently ignore the ability and effort needed to integrate after the sale. Accordingly, your due diligence effort should analyze what's required to integrate the businesses and their assets. It should also include discovering and comparing the two companies' cultural elements, such as beliefs and values, quality of workforce and leadership, work styles, and motivators. For this reason and others, a human resources professional belongs on your due diligence team.

Stage Three: Initiate the Integration

Initiating the integration is the third phase, and it starts when you announce your sale. It would be easy to assume that your only focus at this time is negotiating terms and conditions of the deal. Assuming that you have an ongoing and integral role going forward, however, this is a crucial time to set the stage for a swift and smooth integration.

Joint Executive Team

Identifying and integrating leadership of the merging organizations is vital to making the merger a success. If you have negotiated a significant role in the integration for yourself and your management, your team will help evaluate key employees and create incentives for those selected to stay. Ideally, you and the buyer commit a joint executive team, including human resources, to develop a set of competencies for leaders of the combined organization. In a full integration, the joint team should start at the top of your company's organization chart and select each level of the merged organization's leadership. At each level of the merged organization, managers should provide the joint team a list of employees to consider for each job. You and they may also consider outside candidates with fresh perspectives, skills, and loyalties.

During this third stage, your business integration planning rises to a higher level of intensity as the two firms allocate resources and set time frames and deadlines. That can be done with the establishment of a management and governing structure in this phase. For larger efforts, this would be a construct such as an Integration Management Office (IMO), as discussed in detail below. Planners need to assess operations in greater detail and test assumptions about synergies and benefits that have guided the merger. They should establish the resources and processes needed to assure adequate integration. Their extent and sophistication depend on the level of integration and the complexity and size of the merging organizations. For the more complex integrations, the plans will dive down function by function and process by process to assess their current state, each interim state, the fully integrated state, and steps to get there. This can be very detailed and consuming work, and we advise bringing in experienced outside resources with methodologies and tools to work with the employees.

Include Integration Access in the Deal

As the date for announcing the sale and merger approaches, your integration planning team must accelerate its preparations. Access to the acquiring organization is desirable, but often is limited at this point. Therefore, the team negotiating your sale also should negotiate access so your integration planning team can be in action between the time the deal is closed and announced. Your team needs to hit the ground running so as to minimize disruption and protect productivity.

When your sale is announced, the need for integration visibly begins to filter to the rest of your organization. Communication planning begins. Cross-company functional teams need to be defined and launched, immediately developing definitions and plans for their areas of the integration project. For instance, human resources planning might include identifying and retaining essential employees and resolving differences in 401k plans and transfers. Other issues, among many, are that marketing departments need to align materials and branding, and sales departments need to determine how to integrate client databases and commission plans.

"Day One Plans"

"Day One Plans" are an excellent means of assuring the smooth launch of your integration, starting on the day after your sale is completed. Day One Plans include everything from services that will be provided to protocols for answering telephones on that first day. They must reinforce messages developed during communication planning and might encompass postings on company Web sites and letters to customers, suppliers, agents, and representatives. Name specific people to answer questions and let all employees know to refer queries to them. You might wish to phone or meet with important customers and suppliers one-on-one. Prepare employee information packets to highlight benefits of the acquisition and include a sheet answering frequently asked questions, the announcing press release, an organization chart, benefits information, and names of people assigned to answer questions. Your integration project scope and timetable should be published.

Stage Four: the Integration Plan in Motion

Although we have suggested preliminary activities and assessments ranging from deciding to sell to picking a buyer and entering negotiations, doing the deal and making it work are two separate ends involving different goals and activities. Like the difference between knowing the oven is hot and actually putting your hand on it, knowing and doing are two different things. Stages four and five of the integration effort take effect after your sale closes. They're dedicated to making the merger and acquisition successful and to moving the new organization, however it's structured, forward. By this time, aggressive and comprehensive due diligence and planning have provided you, your managers, and your integration teams the information and governance structures—such as an Integration Management Office—needed to control the integration process. By now, everyone in both organizations should understand at a high level the acquired and acquiring companies' similarities and differences and how to proceed efficiently and effectively.

The First 100 Days

Stage four encompasses the first 100 days after the deal is signed. Its twin goals are to set a tone of urgency and success and to resolve stakeholders' uncertainty and anxiety. Risk management, conversion testing, process dress rehearsals, and contingency planning all happen during this stage as processes are initially combined and become operational. Short, focused integration plans for the first 100 days can establish the momentum everyone will be looking for.

Examples of 100-day plans include communicating internally the scope and timetable of the integration. To return to an earlier example, aligning marketing materials and branding means, in part, assuring that corporate identity standards for letterheads, stationery, business cards, publications, and the company Web site are prepared, published, and in use. Merger integration teams should be trained and meeting to define more detailed plans in all functional areas that are impacted by the merger.

Organization Structure and Metrics

One of your top priorities in stage four is to define and communicate detailed transitional and post-integration organization structures. The new organization chart will be on top of mind for most employees, as they will want to know exactly where in the new organization they reside. It drives the bonus structure to retain and guide personnel, and it should be communicated as quickly as possible to help concentrate on the business and success of the integration.

Another high priority during stage four is formalizing metrics to measure the tactical integration of the business and achievement of the acquisition's strategic goals. Metrics need to be a balanced combination of the reasonable, inspirational, and aggressive. For example, a strategic goal of the merger may have been to expand distribution channels and reach new geographies. A tactical goal would be to be able to repackage and distribute the combined products to all distribution centers in the United States in 120 days. If you are still involved in the merged entity, you can contribute substantially to setting realistic and meaningful metrics.

Visible Leadership

Overall, leaders and managers of both companies need to be visible in each other's organizations, projecting excitement, confidence, and competence. Stage four is an opportunity to radiate and demonstrate behaviors expected of everyone: a focus on open problem-solving, honest cooperation, and equality between colleagues. Activities such as town hall meetings, roundtables, planning sessions, and Q and A sessions give employees a chance to become acquainted with each other's management styles and businesses.

Stage Five: Full Implementation

Stage five is full implementation. Here, you focus on gaining merger synergies quickly and converting to new standard operations. Although both organizations need to complete integration milestones on time with minimal disruptions, this is an opportunity for everyone to release themselves from the prison of perfectionism. The maxim governing stage five should be "75 percent right and 100 percent fast," instead of "100 percent right now." The integration will evolve into an ongoing process of continuous improvement.

Personnel Transfers

Cross-company personnel transfers further encourage and demonstrate the value of the merger. Many assume this means embedding the acquiring company's executives in your company's ranks. Although that's an excellent way to bring the parent company's culture and business practices into yours, you also can support transfers of your employees to the acquirer's. This strengthens understanding and bonds between the two organizations and demonstrates that career opportunities exist for your people in the merged firms.

Technology Transfer

Sophisticated understanding and use of technology during stage five is important. Best-in-class software systems, such as an Enterprise Resource Planning (ERP) system, have institutionalized superior business practices and processes. Perhaps both firms have equally capable systems and may simply move information between them, or perhaps your company or the acquiring firm has the better system and the merging organizations can implement it. If your company is to remain independent, electronic communication links for reporting information may be the only technology combination necessary.

Winding Down to Business as Usual

Over time, the people, systems, and processes of the merged businesses become stabilized, operations become standardized, and a "new normal" emerges. Stage five of the transition winds down. This is the time to bring lessons learned into the organizational memory of the combined companies and to institutionalize best integration practices. As a result, the new, combined organization will have a business integration tool kit of proven processes and method helpful for similar future efforts.

Integrating two businesses is a complex process, not an event. It has many moving parts and tasks to complete, and some disruption is inevitable. However, it's essential to protect productivity and customer satisfaction and loyalty from as many disruptions as possible. Active planning and aggressive management can keep everyone on track and guide the organization through short-term chaos to long-term rewards.

Managing the Business Integration

On average, business integration can take four to eighteen months or more, and the process must be managed carefully. You should treat the undertaking with respect, rigor, and commitment no matter how long you stay with the business.

You can demonstrate that regard by assuring appropriate governance, leadership, and project management structures are in place. If your merger is complex, the recommendations following in the sections below deserve your consideration. On the other hand, smaller mergers may not need the levels of management suggested there. Customize your integration plan for your situation and look to experts for guidance.

High Level View: Governing Structures

Organizations with a history of growth through acquisition have completed many acquisitions and integrations and may rightfully claim integration skills as core competencies. Most businesses, however, have not and cannot. Those businesses need to impose a governing structure that fits their situation to guide integration from beginning to end (see figure 12.1).

Integration Steering Committee

When your sale and merger closes, a productive first step is to establish an integration steering committee. A strategic group of top executives from both organizations, it sets direction, gives approval, and demonstrates that senior executives are on board. As a level of oversight, it approves appropriate approaches toward the business integration, commits resources, removes obstacles, and resolves issues brought for its review. The committee also provides support and recognition and imparts a sense of urgency and importance to the integration.

When cross-functional teams are established and chartered, the integration steering committee assures they are aligned with goals of the acquisition and not working at cross-purposes. Senior managers who were essential during

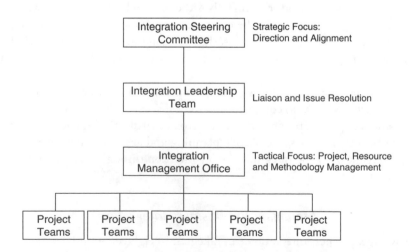

Figure 12.1 Governing Structures for Managing the Integration

your merger negotiations should be members. They know the people and goals guiding the negotiations and merger and can assure consistency throughout the transition.

Integration Leadership Team

Substantial mergers, acquisitions, and integrations may require an integration leadership team that reports to the integration steering committee. It functions more tactically and has hands-on responsibilities for resolving issues before they escalate to the integration steering committee.

Integration Management Office

Reporting to the integration leadership team, in many instances, is a program management office, perhaps more often known as the "integration management office," or IMO. It is *the* central management point for the programs and projects involved in the integration. Regardless of name, it is the overarching tactical management and organizing entity for the entire integration initiative. Anyone should be able to turn to it any time to find the status of any integration project. In complex integrations there could be twenty to twenty-five projects running simultaneously. Bringing in experts with methodologies, tools, and years of experience could be very valuable here. Again, for smaller integrations, the IMO's size and presence could be scaled down. A single integration manager could be "the office."

The IMO is responsible for the day-to-day hard work of making the integration a success. It assures that information is shared, progress is reported, communications are effective, risks are mitigated, and issues are tracked to resolution. It defines, designs, and manages all cross-functional teams, determines they are properly and consistently trained, and evaluates their proposals for projects and resources. Its chief focal points are process, communication, and management. It is the one place where all integration projects roll up into the master business integration plan and where management gets an update regarding progress at any time.

Creating Integration Teams, Plans, and Deliverables

The integration management office defines and installs cross-functional teams (such as communication) and function-specific teams (such as our earlier examples of human resources, marketing, or sales). Team leaders will be responsible for day-to-day activities and deliverables. They have the responsibility not just for creating and executing detailed plans and deliverables but also for creating momentum and commitment within each integration team.

Team leaders should choose members for their expertise and ability to work well in potentially ambiguous and usually demanding circumstances as decisions and changes are made. Each team needs to refine its required deliverables and activities pertinent to its charter, then further break them down into individual projects with project plans.

Begin at the End

Most often, arriving at detailed project plans begins by understanding the current state and desired end for each function at both companies. When your sale was closed, the new organization's structure was designed. To implement that design via detailed projects, teams must reason through the actual changes and supporting activities and tasks necessary to effect those changes.

The first task is to compare both companies' organization charts and how the current scheme differs from the one desired at the integration's end. The next step in documenting the current situation is to assess its people (including job titles and locations), work, systems, standards, communications, and tools. Transition project activities and tasks are the actions that achieve the desired end. During complex transitions, teams may have to establish interim states of transition. Documenting risks and mitigation strategies, synergies, best practices, and related matters may also become necessary project tasks.

When duplicate departments are to be combined, some consulting firms believe it is a best practice to bring in both departments to discuss how to operate going forward and evaluate all job positions. We have found that this does not work. There is too much at stake for everyone in that room to be unbiased and produce the best solution. Instead, the highest-ranking people of those departments should meet, design the job structures, best practices, and fill in the gaps.

Roll-Up

These detailed project plans are then rolled into a master integration plan directed by the integration management office. Project teams send their status reports, issues logs, and deliverables to the integration management office. These are a visible accounting of the integration's progress and also of dependencies, constraints, and conflicts among subprojects. Status meetings and reports are standard for tracking performance integration projects and their progress. They are usually scheduled weekly to review progress, share information, and create mutual understanding. The integration management office is the focal point for all integration activities and the conduit for passing issues upward to the integration management team. Again, a single person might serve as the integration management office in less complex integrations.

Accountability and Cooperation

Once project plans are developed and team members are assigned tasks, individual accountability can be measured. Like any major initiative, individual performance needs to be measured. Change is deceptively difficult, and many mergers fail because of people issues. Employees must be motivated to cooperate and achieve merger objectives.

Senior managers who were involved in negotiating the acquisition likely have strong knowledge of the merged entity and its relationships. Managers at lower organizational levels, however, likely do not, and therefore may adopt protectionist attitudes. As business integration teams carry out their work, they build cooperative relationships at all levels.

Human resources has an important role in achieving a successful transition through its tools for stimulating the integration and sustaining business productivity. For example, it can deconstruct goals of the acquisition and integration into employee performance requirements that become the basis for employees' performance appraisals, incentive compensation, and rewards.

Communication

Communication planning is important for retaining employees, suppliers, and customers, and for motivating their acceptance of the new, combined firm. The selling owner should participate, if possible, in communication planning as someone who knows these important constituencies and how to shape and deliver messages to them. The purpose of the communication plan is to convey—immediately after the deal's announcement—what will change and what will not. The merger will raise questions about the new organization's structures, roles, responsibilities, and reporting relationships. The human impact—what about my job and benefits?—will be of highest interest to everyone. If not informed speedily, people will make uninformed assumptions and miscalculations that distract them from their work and reduce their productivity. A communications plan is, therefore, also a "productivity protection plan," and has been discussed in more detail in an earlier chapter.

One recommendation we've see implemented successfully is the appointment of "ambassadors" for each functional area from each company. These people attend monthly calls with executive sponsors where they bring questions from and return answers to their area, thereby assuring everyone is educated on a series of merger-related topics. An example topic would be how annual recognition will be handled going forward. They are usually an hour-and-a-half long, with one hour for education, and half an hour for Q and A.

Above all, be honest. Although this may seem obvious, we know of a situation where the seller was not honest with his employees, and the buyer asked him to leave the merged firm early as a result. Although the seller and buyer had met and agreed on messages to be delivered, he did not deliver them. In this case, the seller told his employees that it was a merger of equals, that no one would lose their jobs, and that they would continue to do business the way they always had. None of this was true. Was he trying to save face or be a hero? What did he think would happen when the truth came out? Clearly this is not a situation you would ever want to be in. If there is unpleasant news to deliver, the buyer and seller should agree on what messages should be delivered, and deliver them quickly and honestly.

Conclusion

A successful sale and merger doesn't end with a sale, nor, really, does it end with a merger. It takes a long time for two entities to determine and institutionalize the new normal. And a sale and merger is truly successful only if the merger is successful. Making it successful involves an extensive process of transition before and after the merger is final. If you sell your business to another business, you must be committed to success of the acquisition whether you leave the business or remain in some capacity. Aside from that being the right and professional thing to do, your commitment will help the business's viability in the long term. Most selling business owners want to be involved in integrating the business and contribute to its success in its new form.

As a whole, the business integration process starts with discovering and building a common understanding of two organizations' similarities and differences. With the benefit of comparative analysis earlier and with acquisition and integration goals at hand, management can decide whether processes and functions should be left in place, consolidated for operational efficiencies, or integrated for maximum leverage. If management and employees are receptive to finding new ways of operating, the result may be a wave of organizational innovation and a brighter future for the acquired and acquiring companies.

Takeaway Lessons

- Merging your firm with another after sale is a more intricate and extended undertaking than merely selling it. When you're acquired, your sale is not truly successful until your firm is integrated successfully with the buyer's. If you intend to sell to an acquirer, the goal of a successful integration should guide your deliberations and actions at each stage of your selling process.
- Integration is a five-stage process that begins with due diligence, expresses itself in each phase of your sale process, and becomes intensive after the sale is complete. You need to think constantly about integration when conducting your sale process and assure that process includes deliberations needed to make the integration work. Among the encyclopedia of items to hold in mind are choosing a buyer with whom you can integrate well, assuring access to your buyer's organization and managers before the sale is complete, and forming joint integration committees between the two organizations.
- Successful sale and integration of larger companies requires an operational structure that is staggering in its scope and detail. Depending upon the size of the integration, you will need a strategic steering committee, a leadership group, and a tactical manager. Each higher level of the integration

management structure must guide and facilitate the work of the lower, and teams established for each must operate with a defined charter and assigned duties having specific metrics of achievement. Smaller mergers require less management overhead, of course, but need to be vigilantly overseen as well.

• Above all, your sale-merger-integration is communication-intensive. During the earliest stages of the sale, you naturally will restrict information about negotiations and the impending sale, but even during this silent period you will be assessing who needs to be told what, when, and how. You must develop the right message and media for communicating with everyone touched by the merger, ranging from employees to communities where you operate, and roll out your communications appropriately. Your mentality will be as important as the right message and medium. Your communications need to be honest, forthright, accurate, and encouraging in order to earn support for the merger from managers, employees, customers, suppliers, and shareholders.

For additional resources and tools, visit www.sellingyourbusinessformore.com

CHAPTER 13

After the Close: Now What?

Introduction

If you've followed this book's suggestions, you've taken time to think about where your life after selling your business could lead. You may have given concrete form to your post-sale dreams or at least sketched the outlines of your future. You now face a new realization: you have a whole new array of decisions to make.

For one thing, you suddenly have a large sum of cash instead of the substantial illiquid wealth represented by your business. That cash is a very tangible realization of your years of hard work and dedication, and you should deploy it responsibly and productively.

What's more, you might no longer have access to people who usually helped you to make such big decisions. You may have turned to your CFO and others in your former company for expert advice on personal financial matters. They may even have lent a hand in preparing tax returns for you and your spouse and your children. Once your business has passed to the new owner, they and their help might no longer be available when you need it more than ever.

You no longer carry the responsibility of ownership and the day-to-day obligations of management. You are freed from worries about next month's cash flow, how to energize your sales force, or how to tweak a new product to perfection. But where there were huge demands on your time and a rigorous daily schedule, now there's no place you have to be and no structure to your day or week. And no outlet for your passion to create, to nurture, and to build.

If members of your family were involved in owning or managing your company, a good portion of their identity may have vanished. They may feel they "used to be somebody." Your business may have been the centerpiece of your family's legacy to a community or to succeeding generations. It may also have been the center of their social life, the place where they first met their wife or husband and still have lifelong friends. Now a piece of their social fabric has been torn away.

For those reasons or others, some family members or former partners may be deeply upset or thrown off balance by the implications of this major life change. Their continuing distress may have far-reaching effects on the stability and emotional health of your family system.

These very real and common shifts in your life after sale demand your attention. This chapter offers some suggestions on what steps to take.

From Owner to Investor

Significant wealth brings new responsibilities and obligations. You have just transitioned from owner to investor, and just as you were the steward of the family business you will now be the steward of the family wealth. You will need to choose a wealth management firm to help you make the right plans for investments, which will safeguard and grow your wealth while providing income and liquidity to satisfy your lifestyle. Investing large sums of money is not a do-it-yourself project—here is where you call in professionals. Just as you were the expert on your business, you want to find the right set of experts to handle your investment matters.

Types of Firms

The number of firms offering investment and asset management services is dizzying, and over the past ten years each has expanded its products and services to the extent that they all seem to offer much the same services. In fact, there's a profound difference among providers, and it's worthwhile to do your own due diligence to find the right wealth manager for your goals and preferences. Broadly speaking, there are three types of investment and wealth management firms you might want to investigate.

Brokerage Houses

A *brokerage house* is an investment firm that is essentially an intermediary that puts buyers and sellers together to facilitate transactions. Today most are *broker-dealers*. A broker trades for clients; a dealer trades as a principal for the firm's account and can resell securities owned by the firm to clients. Professionals must have at least a Series 7 license and often have other certifications, such as Chartered Financial Analyst.

Most brokerage houses today offer both *trading accounts* and *wrap* or *advisory accounts*. A *trading account* is one that holds marketable securities that you can buy or sell at your discretion. Your broker may offer advice on particular securities but doesn't usually offer a "big picture" strategy. In a trading account, you will be charged a commission on each transaction, and the broker is not prohibited from recommending that you buy securities his or her firm has purchased as a dealer in its own account for resale to customers. That is not necessarily a bad thing—they may be very good securities—but you should be aware of the possible bias.

A *wrap* or *advisory account* will offer a personal investment advisor who will design your asset allocation strategy and select funds, managers, and securities for you to meet that strategy. These accounts usually carry an annual fee based on the value of the securities in your account.

This type of wealth manager is insured by the Securities Investor Protection Corporation (SIPC), which protects clients if the brokerage firm is forced into bankruptcy. Covered losses are insured up to $500,000 per account.

The largest of these firms have built out capabilities to offer a broad range of both marketable and nonmarketable investments that may be managed either in-house or by specialty managers with other firms. Many also provide financial planning, investment banking services, and other specialized products.

Asset Management Firms

These money managers are firms that are focused primarily on managing the assets of high net-worth individuals. They range in size from small boutiques with a handful of investment professionals to large firms with many divisions and extensive investment offerings. Most of these firms also have a broker-dealer affiliate to process their transactions. Asset management firms will offer an identification of your investment objectives and risk tolerance and design asset allocation and investment strategy accordingly. Smaller firms will have some professionals who manage stock and bond portfolios directly, and they may have access to a network that allows them to invest your funds with managers outside the firm.

The larger firms will have a broad choice of in-house products from mutual funds to tailored domestic and global stock and bond portfolios, alternative categories, and tax-advantaged funds. They may also offer an extensive array of service in addition to investment products, including in-house equity research, personal financial planning, retirement planning, investment banking, and option and derivative strategies. They are active managers but will have access to wealth managers from other firms to optimize your diversification and will provide oversight and ongoing recommendations for your portfolios.

Accounts are insured in most cases by the SIPC, but may have privately underwritten excess insurance to provide more protection on your account. Annual fees will be calculated on the value of your assets under management.

Banks with Private Wealth Management Services

Many large banks have comprehensive and sophisticated services for high-net-worth individuals and their families. They will have a great deal of in-house investment capability, offering separately managed domestic and foreign equity and fixed-income portfolios across a variety of styles. Their investment offerings will be broad and similar to the range of products you might find in the large brokerage houses or large investment management firms. Many banks, these days, have "open architecture" programs to provide access to top-tier managers outside of the bank as well. You will find programs for alternative assets and funds-of-funds plus special asset management (real estate, family business, oil and gas). Unlike brokerage houses, however, banks also have traditional banking services for individuals and corporations and extensive trust and estate services. In their wealth management practice they will fully integrate trust and estate plans and concerns, investment management, oversight and financial planning, and banking.

Your investment portfolios will be held in a separate account with assets titled in the name of each account, and you may have protection in those accounts against fraud or certain kinds of loss other than market fluctuation. A bank will charge annual fees for investment management services based on the value of the assets in your account.

As providers continually add more choice and complexity of investments to their investment management services, differences among these three types of providers become more blurred. Today, there are far greater differences between a small firm of any type and a larger full-service organization. Your choice should also rest in part on whether you need integrated services across a number of financial areas—for example, investments, trust and estate services, financial planning, and special asset management.

To identify the best candidates, seek referrals from your business and professional network. Ask your sales team specialists, your trustees, and your financial planner. Your estate planner, your corporate attorney, and accountant will have had dealings with a variety of private wealth management providers and can introduce you to the best contenders.

How to Select the Right Wealth Manager

Your wealth management provider will take a prominent place alongside your other trusted advisors, so be sure to choose one that is capable, thorough, and sensitive to your needs and preferences over the years.

Investment Experience and the Firm's Capabilities

For starters, you want an investment firm that specializes in managing wealth of the size you're about to realize from your sale. If you will receive $50 to $75 million, for example, ask prospective candidates how many of their clients entrust them with a similar quantity of investable assets. In particular, you'll want to know if firms offer a broad menu of investment products. You want access to separately managed funds across both equity and fixed-income assets, and you want a firm that provides exposure to alternative investments like real estate, hedge funds, and private equity—usually in a fund-of-funds structure.

The best managers among all categories of investment firms today offer "open architecture"—that is, the firm can give you access to best-in-class managers outside the firm in addition to expert investment managers within the firm. Open architecture gives you the widest choices for composing the most effective financial team for your assets.

If you expect a larger sum—perhaps $400 to $500 million—at the close of your sale, you want the firm you choose to have many clients in similar situations. If it does, you may be more confident that the firm is conversant with the sophisticated and ever-emerging strategies for managing such substantial wealth effectively. Besides offering open architecture, the management firm should be staffed by experts in alternative assets that round out the equity/fixed income diversification with hedge, private equity, and venture capital, commodities and other specialty categories. These specialty programs may require help from outside consultants, but your wealth management firm must be accustomed to integrating those special investments in a sizable portfolio within an appropriate, comprehensive plan.

Specialized Expertise

The firm you choose also should be conversant with creating and managing investment partnerships and limited liability companies. A family fortunate enough to enjoy substantial wealth usually will keep it in a variety of financial "pockets." Those commonly include family trusts or trusts for the benefit of grandchildren, a pool of funds that you or your spouse own outright or in a living trust, or other family entities or partnerships. If you broke up the ownership of your company before selling, some of your former financial vehicles may now be comprised largely of cash. Your planning team may recommend using partnerships to consolidate these smaller pools into one or several larger pools. Doing so may enable you to manage the assets more economically and to hire quality investment managers whose minimum investment thresholds differ.

If you've received stock of a public company in exchange for your business, be sure your wealth management advisor has experience managing single-stock strategies. He or she should be able to advise you on the intricacies of managing and liquidating restricted stock and know how to mitigate risks of having wealth concentrated in a single company.

Performance History

Ask your investment firm candidates for a performance history relative to relationships similar to yours. You want the firm you select to have generated solid investment returns for clients like you over many years. Remember that short-term performance is not necessarily a good indicator of ability.

Insurance and Protection

Ask each candidate to explain exactly how your assets are protected and what insurance arrangement they have. Ask, for example, if they are a member of SPIC and whether they carry additional insurance protection. Some arrangements protect you only in the case of the insolvency of the investment firm. Others will protect you against fraud or other causes of loss. No one protects you against loss due to market fluctuations.

Risk and Mitigation

Let's take a moment to discuss the possible risks you take when you place your assets with a third party and how you can best minimize or eliminate them. In the recent past, we have seen media reports concerning the conviction of renowned investment manager Bernie Madoff for executing a twenty-year Ponzi scheme that defrauded clients of $50 billion, leaving scores of elderly retirees penniless and destitute and others fleeced of large portions of their life savings. At about the same time Madoff's scheme was discovered, prominent Texas financier and banker Allen Stanford was charged with massive fraud for allegedly bilking clients out of $8 billion in yet another Ponzi scheme. Both Madoff and Stanford had been extremely well respected and revered for their professional successes prior to these events. Bernie Madoff had been the chairman of NASDAQ, and Allen Stanford was knighted by the countries of Barbuda and Antigua in 2006.

How do you avoid being inadvertently caught up in such a devastating circumstance when you entrust others to manage your money? There are several important points to keep in mind.

- Diversification is paramount. Your pool of assets should never be invested entirely in one strategy or with a single manager. It is safe to hire a firm that will provide investment management oversight over a group of managers, but if you do, be sure the managers chosen to run the underlying funds are appropriately separate and not affiliated. Some high-net-worth families identify two institutions to manage their wealth, so there is diversification even at that level.
- Be sure that due diligence has been performed by you, your in-house investment advisor, or your hired institutional investment professional to assure the following with respect to underlying investment managers or funds:
  — Confirm that securities traded by the subject manager are traded through a third-party broker-dealer, not affiliated with that subject manager.
  — Confirm that securities held in accounts for clients are in the custody of an independent professional custodian (bank or financial service institution) that isn't affiliated with the manager.

— Find out who audits the manager's books. It should be at least a midsize CPA firm with a respectable reputation.

— Ask questions until you're satisfied you understand the strategy employed by managers you may select. Be sure your investment professionals understand the strategy and confirm that it is reasonable and that the reported performance history is plausible.

Setting Expectations and Goals

The firm you select will spend time with you at the outset of your relationship to understand your goals and objectives for the wealth you entrust to their care. You will provide documents, background information, and preferences so that together with you and your planning team your wealth advisor can identify an objective for each pool of funds to be managed. These objectives will delineate the balance between income and capital appreciation appropriate for each account, partnership, or trust. This will be the basis of the broad guidelines for the asset allocation design.

The framework for the different categories of investments that should make up your portfolio is its *asset allocation*. Once guidelines for the categories of assets are set, your advisor will recommend specific managers or funds for each category. A more comprehensive and integrated view may also be applied to assure that the overall investment strategy across multiple pools is in fact integrated appropriately. For example, the manager will review the asset allocations, separately and collectively, for all accounts or trusts that benefit each child or grandchild to assure those accounts are serving all the objectives set for that child.

Reporting

The wealth management firm you choose should send monthly or quarterly reports showing how your managers are performing compared to their respective benchmarks. Your firm's team should meet with you at least once a year to discuss how your investments are performing and to review your asset allocation. You will want to assure that your asset allocation is still appropriate or if it needs altering because of market conditions or changes in your preferences. If there are weak performers among managers in your portfolio, your firm will discuss with you whether to change managers or give them more time.

Personal Guidance

You have spent a good deal of your life with your wealth tied up in a single asset. You were comfortable with this concentrated investment in your company because you were in control and you knew its risks and opportunities intimately. The prospect of taking your cash proceeds and investing in a diverse array of marketable securities of companies over which you have no control may seem very daunting and highly risky. You would not be the first entrepreneur who felt that way.

Therefore, you should choose a wealth manager who will guide you through the fundamentals of modern portfolio theory and explain why a careful asset allocation protects your return and diminishes your risks. You want your questions answered seriously and patiently. You want an advisor who will teach, not preach. If you have concerns, you want an advisor who will not pressure you into a direction you don't want to take.

If you are seriously uncomfortable with market investments, you want to have a manager who moves conservatively at your pace toward a fully diversified portfolio. One example we have seen was a business owner who sold his business for several hundred million dollars. Although a widely diversified portfolio would have been prescribed for such a pool of wealth, he asked that his cash be initially invested entirely in Treasury securities, a secure, low-risk strategy. Over the ensuing months and years, he agreed with his wealth advisors to move capital slowly into stocks of large U.S. companies, then into smaller companies, and then into bonds with longer-term maturities. After several more years, he entered into real estate, private equity, and venture capital funds and other classes of investments until his asset allocation was more broadly diversified.

Comfort and Fit

Just as you did when choosing advisors and specialists for your selling team, choose your investment professionals based on "comfort factors" as well as their prominence and expertise. You must feel you can work easily with them, discuss investment choices and strategies when *you* are available, and have your questions answered as they arise. Financial institutions and wealth management firms understand the importance of the right "fit" between client and manager. If you are uncertain that a person assigned to your relationship will work out, explain what you're looking for and ask to meet another candidate.

Replacement Service Provider

As owner and operator of your own company, you, like most business owners, probably called on the financial and tax expertise of your CFO or controller's division to help with personal financial matters. Many closely held businesses do some tax preparation, tax planning, and even financial planning for the founder and family. As the family ascends into multiple generations and the business expands, sometimes staffing within the business expanded to handle these duties. Some CFOs become such trusted advisors that they help with estate planning for multiple generations within the family. Perhaps the company's controller takes care of bill-paying for an infirm grandmother, or its sales manager finds tickets for a sports event or concert. In multigenerational businesses, sometimes executives or plant managers take over educating the next generation to succeed in the business.

If your company resources helped you and your family in such ways, you will need to replace these critical services once you sell. Moreover, the fact of the sale will beget issues that you must address and manage in some new fashion. Even if you have selected a wealth management firm, someone has to perform oversight, scrutinize reports, and manage the manager.

After the infusion of liquid wealth, your estate and tax planning and that of your spouse and children will be more complex. You will want financial and tax planning to integrate the concerns and preferences of multiple generations. Your children and grandchildren will have to be educated in the issues associated with a legacy of wealth—financial planning, asset management, philanthropy. Some may benefit from coaching on how to design meaning into their lives when there's no need to work for a living. If there are trusts in your wealth plan, fiduciary issues must be managed and integrated into everyone's concerns and objectives.

A Family Office

The solution for most wealthy families is a *family office* (FO), a private company owned and controlled by a single family to oversee and manage its financial, philanthropic, and personal matters.

Typically, the FO does not directly make investments. But it does manage total asset allocation and investment strategy for all family holdings, select managers, and review their performance, often with help of outside investment firms and consultants. The FO will administer family investment or tax planning entities, including family partnerships and limited liability companies. Some employ accountants to prepare tax returns and do partnership accounting; others hire and manage an outside accountant.

Experts in an FO can help with complex financial planning, including life insurance analysis and philanthropic planning. They may rework debt structure with bank financing for family members and their various accounts. Families with substantial wealth are more inclined to invest a portion of their portfolios in alternatives assets such as venture capital, hedge funds, private equity, and commodity funds. Professionals in the FO may be proficient at the selection oversight of these singular asset types.

Most important, the FO coordinates cash flow and distributions to family members, investments, management of nonfinancial assets, and financial and multigenerational wealth transfer planning. The family office is there to do whatever it takes in any realm and should be responsive to family members' questions and requests. If they do not have the expertise in-house, family office managers will find a provider who does.

When a family enters a new charitable or business enterprise, the FO effectively runs it. Affluent families may own yachts, airplanes, or collectible autos.

The FO is there to help, whether in building the yacht, managing the airplanes, or making sure the autos are in excellent condition and fully insured. Often, the FO includes a real estate specialist who can help buy and sell homes and manage their upkeep, taxes, and domestic employees for a plethora of primary residences, ranches, and vacation homes.

As you expect from the lengthy responsibilities and the skill, experience, and caliber of employees necessary to fulfill them, family offices are expensive. According to a survey of Family Office Exchange members, the cost ranges from $300,000 to $3 million each year. If you are considering your own FO, enlist your trusted advisors and organizations like the Family Office Exchange to help you design and staff the right facility for your family. We have seen many highly competent CFO's turn to heading up and helping to build a private family office.

Multifamily Offices

Unless you have $200 million in investable assets, your best choice may be a *multifamily office*—an FO serving more than one family. Multifamily offices initially were outgrowths of FOs that saw economies of scale in devoting their expensive infrastructure to serve several families. More recently, small groups of professionals with the requisite specialized skills founded multifamily offices. Banks and brokerage houses with affluent clientele have opened multifamily offices within their private wealth practices.

Many multifamily offerings offer a robust variety of services, including concierge services, lifestyle management and coaching, and wealth education for children and family. They may also offer business advisory, real estate advisory, or oil-gas-mineral expertise to support entrepreneurial endeavors in those areas.

Your New Focus and Your Family Legacy

Your family business is gone, but can and should you launch a family enterprise to take its place as the central focus of your family? The wealth provided to you and other owners or shareholders after selling your business offers both the financial wherewithal and the freedom to choose how to use it. Your family or co-owners may be willing and eager to invest a portion of their newfound wealth and to collaborate on new ventures.

If you and your family members or former partners decide to start a new enterprise or multiple enterprises, whatever they might be, you will present everyone a chance to build upon and extend the legacy you've created together. You offer your family a new focal point that may engage many members at different tasks and levels, but will promote family harmony to be working collaboratively with a single purpose.

Charitable Foundations

Perhaps you and your family have always been involved with your place of worship or a charity or an organization you're committed to. Or perhaps you've always meant to become involved, but until now you lacked the time and funds to make a contribution and a difference. In either case, you may be interested in creating your own charitable foundation. Launching your own foundation might be more than an opportunity to immerse yourselves in good works. By creating a new, tangible mission for the family to support, you might reestablish the sense of unity and purpose that your business provided.

If your family has no clear or long-standing preference for the kinds of philanthropic endeavors you'd like to support, call everyone together and discuss the nearly infinite number of involvements that might interest everyone. If there's no group consensus about what to support, perhaps you could establish several separate foundations. Consider writing a family mission statement to clarify what you as a family think is important in deciding how to apportion your charitable funds. You might offer leadership and trustee roles in the family foundation to those who would like to replace their lost family business posts. Or you may have siblings or children who don't have strong business training and didn't participate in your business, but have strong interpersonal skills and expertise in the arts, education, or social services.

Be sure to seek the advice of a charitable planning professional to set up your charitable entity in the most effective manner. A professional can outline the many tax-advantaged strategies for establishing a family foundation and discuss different types of entities to accomplish what you'd like to do.

Entrepreneurial Enterprises

You've spent the better part of your life building a successful business. You are a capable and proven entrepreneur. Why not use your knowledge, judgment, and insight in an enterprise that fosters entrepreneurship in others? You could join with your former business owners or family in contributing cash directly to early-stage venture companies, perhaps in the industry you just left. You might take a hands-on approach to those investment companies, sitting on their boards, helping to develop growth plans, bringing in new investors, and even using your network to help them expand through strategic partnerships.

Real Estate Development

If venture capital funding doesn't appeal to you, perhaps you prefer to find one good company to buy and build. In our experience, many people in your situation involve themselves in real estate.

A real estate enterprise of some type is often a logical choice. Like many business owners, you may have had a substantial real estate component to your business. If you owned a hospitality company, for example, which routinely purchased land and built out a new hotel with an accompanying restaurant and retail space, or if you developed your own production and warehousing facilities for a manufacturing company, you may be a candidate to pursue real estate development.

Real Estate Management

Or perhaps real estate management is more your cup of tea, because you and your partners managed many of your commercial properties yourselves. When your properties held more square footage than your operation required, perhaps you managed to find the right leasing candidates and were directly involved in structuring and negotiating leases. You may be exceedingly familiar with real estate markets and the ebb and flow of commercial demand in areas of the country where you did business.

Land-Based Business

Sometimes a land-based business evolves naturally into other real estate initiatives. In the American Southeast during the 1980s and 1990s, for example, timberland and farming operations often were located in the growth path of a nearby city. Their land holdings attracted interest from developers who envisioned residential communities, office parks, and shopping malls sprouting up on them. If you were in a similar situation as a business owner, you might decide to partner with an expert or to take on the risk of development yourself. We've seen many owners move into real estate development, leasing, or management as a way of creating a new business focus after selling a business.

Repairing Family Disruptions

No matter what the financial rewards, sale of your business is life-changing and often threatening—especially to some stakeholders and family members more than others. This is understandable. The business had provided an income, a routine, a purpose, and sometimes prestige, all of which may have vanished in the transfer of ownership. Perhaps some family members and partners never fully agreed to the sale in the first place. Or perhaps they never thought the sale would turn out as it did. Their discontent can turn the fruits of your labor into bitter fruit, so it's worth doing what you can to relieve it.

One possibility is to offer unhappy relatives and former partners roles in the newly founded family foundation or other enterprise. Certainly, continuing communication and expressions of understanding on your part may be helpful. But if the discontent escalates, perhaps even threatens a family schism, call in professional help. Family counselors may be able to resolve or at least diminish the anger. Often, however, anger and unhappiness following the sale of the business are merely emotions displaced from earlier, long-smoldering issues. Personal psychological attention may be needed, and the person who's been closest for many years—the person who's shared the toil and the success of building a business—may be the one who should offer the suggestion.

Conclusion

No matter how well you've planned for your life after sale, that first day you no longer have to be in the office can present a cold moment of realization. It also is a day that opens wide prospects and enormous potential for your future and that of your family and former associates. To make the most of everything that life after sale offers, you need to understand the kind of transitions you've just made—from owner to investor, from provider to steward, from former entrepreneur to philanthropist, and many others.

As when starting and building your business, you need sound counsel to build and direct your new life. You want a wealth advisor who is experienced and offers a range of alternatives that meet your temperament and need for the broadest diversification. The same is true for other aspects of your post-sale life, whether you're establishing a family foundation or venture capital enterprise or starting another new firm. It can be especially true if not everyone among your personal or business family is on an even keel after the sale.

The concluded sale of your business is an end and a beginning. When the ink dries on your contract, the page clears for many new chapters ahead. You are the author.

Takeaway Lessons

- Your best foresight and perfect execution produce an ideal sale, and everything still can change when the deal is done. When your role as business owner ends, your role in your family, community, and friendships inevitably changes. Before your sale commences and as it unfolds, you need to be pondering what might be different, desirable, or even dispiriting in your altered roles.
- The end of your role as an owner can be the beginning of invigorating and worthwhile endeavors, whether in another business, as an advisor sponsor of other entrepreneurs, or as a philanthropist. Those endeavors, too, need to be pondered and planned and, if need be, they may also need to include the involvement of former partners of many kinds.
- Selling your business liberates the liquidity you've had tied up in your firm—sometimes very substantial amounts of it. Liquid wealth needs to be reapportioned productively and responsibly, and that means picking the right investment management firm as well as other professionals, such as those who run family offices, to help. In picking these advisors, you will examine

their experience with accounts of your size and especially their access to the full plethora of financial vehicles needed for proper diversification. You will examine their historical performance, insist on senior representation from the firm's professionals, and select a primary advisor who is sensitive to your risk preferences and compatible with your overall temperament.

• As an owner, you may have used the professional resources of your business in personal financial matters, and those resources may no longer be available to you. In addition, the responsibilities of sizable wealth—and your choice of a post-sale endeavor—may mean you need extra help. One way to replace former services and acquire new expertise is by contracting a family office or multifamily office to assist you.

For additional resources and tools, visit www.sellingyourbusinessformore.com

Conclusion and Congratulations

Congratulations for building a successful business to the point where you can consider selling it. What you've done to date—creating jobs and bringing value to your market—is a remarkable testament to your vision, values, and hard work. You can now look to pass your business and its opportunities to someone new and enjoy the rewards that come with your success. Our time with you in this book, sharing our experiences and asking tough questions, is just a starting point. As the family business legend Estee Lauder said:

> The schools and the books make it all seem so cut and dried. If you do this, you get this. Well, that's wrong. Just as a mother comes to know and work with her toddler, an executive comes to know the special vagaries and unique sensibilities of her business and of her own inner voice that tells the truth—if she listens hard enough. It's a delicate business, business is, and I never yet met anyone who learned her business from a book or school, just as I never met a mother who raised a wonderful child from a book. Each business person must find a style, that voice that grows clearer and louder with each success and failure. Observing your own and your competitor's successes and failures makes your inner business voice more sure and vivid.

An Ivy League education or a well-written book—even ours—cannot give you everything you need to be successful at building a business or selling it. The intricacies and special circumstances of your company's success are known best by you, not professors or authors. Our goal through this book is to encourage you toward your own holistic view of your sale, respectful of the knowledge you bring to the business, and a framework broader than just the transaction. We seek to give you the foundation to "listen hard enough" to your business and yourself to create a whole-person process of selling your business—a process that fits right for you and everyone you care about.

Just as each reader's company and situation are unique, each reader is at a different place in the selling process. Perhaps you are wrestling with the decision to sell and trying to find that compelling reason that propels you to make such a significant change. Or perhaps the decision has been thrust upon you by your partners, circumstances, or someone else's desire for change. You, the business, or the market may not be ready. And since owning your business is so much more than any job could be, it can be difficult to design that "next big thing" that will fulfill you as your business has. Not having that defined has made many business owners hesitate to sell when they should have. Having a driving reason to sell and a compelling future vision with all owners working toward the same goal are necessary to complete the hard work of setting you and the business free to grow and enter your next stages.

Your foundation for decision-making should be your values and your definition of success financially, personally and for your business. As author and success coach Brian Tracy points out, successful people are intensely action-oriented. So taking time out to reflect on your own future is probably an unfamiliar experience for you. What do you want this new destination to be? To articulate your values clearly is to discover what your guiding principles—your roadmap—will be throughout your selling process. Do you want to stay with the business, and if so, in what role and for how long? Once you leave, what will you do, and how will you finance it? Your answers to all of those questions and many others will influence why and how you sell your business, what you sell it for, and to whom.

This change will be both an ending and a beginning for everyone involved. While it presents opportunity, it also portends loss. Loss is a difficult emotion to contend with, but a sense of loss can influence the business negatively if you do not understand, respect, and handle it wisely. The entire selling process is complex. It layers additional responsibilities and tasks on people who already are juggling many of both. You must enter that process prepared to invest the resources and to create the structures needed to manage it. Not only should you invest in improvements that will enhance the valuation of your business, but you also need to invest in the transferability of your business. Part of that transferability includes moving your responsibilities to the new owner, remembering that while your business is now second nature to you, it won't be to your successor. Understanding, planning, and communicating the change start with you and will ripple throughout your organization. Someday in the not-too-distant future, you will have to pass the torch. It is your job to see that everyone is ready for that day.

Different sellers have different time frames for leaving their business. There is a tradeoff between time and price: if you can spend the time preparing and improving the business, that could very well be reflected in a higher selling price and greater funding for your desired post-sale life. Given your time frame and the market, you should prioritize your efforts and investments for maximum and rapid impact. You never know when the right buyers will show up, and you want to be ready for them. This could mean recalibrating your board, building your management team, showing the true profitability of the business, following the money when improving processes and cash flow, and preparing the documentation buyers will want to see. All of this requires that you simultaneously keep your business running, growing, and profitable, yet manage the important sale initiatives. Bringing in experienced outside help will be extremely beneficial.

Almost all business owners we have dealt with have already set in their minds the price they want for their business. As the Greek poet Antiphanes said in the fourth century B.C., "A merchant has high hopes for windfalls—of which sometimes the wind holds total control." Unfortunately, a price you have in mind based on dated market conditions, general rules of thumb, book value, or hearing what a competitor received, may be unrealistic. Your best course of action is to use some or all of the three common professional expressions of valuation: fair market value, strategic value, and multiples of EBITDA. You should understand the principles behind each valuation because they affect the transaction and have an impact on taxation and donations. Overall, strategic buyers are usually the most attractive, because they're willing to pay top dollar for efficiencies or synergies your business will bring them. But, in the end, the market at that point in time is the final arbiter of your business's value.

Although we've been saying throughout this book that your business is more than just money, handling your money wisely is still extraordinarily important. Trusts are one vehicle to make sure that you keep more of it. The rules around trusts and taxes are intricate and ever-changing, so summoning knowledgeable counsel early into the process is essential. To provide well for yourself, family, heirs, and charitable interests, you should begin considering these legal and financial issues right now and substantially before you put your company up for sale. This is the liquidity event you have been waiting for, and you absolutely want to make the most of it. And your values should again be a guiding voice throughout the planning process.

Financial and legal advisors who help you keep more of your post-sale rewards are merely parts of the full team you should engage. Pairing your knowledgeable internal business team with specialized, experienced outside experts will be needed to see the entire selling process to its successful conclusion. Outside experts, including a senior investment banker, transaction attorney, and external auditor will work with your internal team to prepare documents and negotiate your sale. Some consultants specialize in ESOPs, MBOs, recapitalizations, earnouts, and stock-for-stock sales, and you must include them if your transaction includes those possibilities. Whatever you're considering, get the right help. And be vigilant in assuring that your internal and external teams are the equal match of your buyer's teams and can represent you well on an equal footing.

There are many twists and turns to navigate on your way to a successful sale. Creating harmony and congruence among owners, family members, and other stakeholders can be difficult. So is striking the right balance between involvement and authority. But everyone must be on the same team to win the game. Don't be afraid to bring in mediators and specialists who have guided those previously in your position.

As a general rule, the process of selling your business has five steps: contacting buyers, developing interest among them, evaluating offers, negotiating, and closing. How your process is structured—a broad or limited auction, targeted-buyer campaign, or some combination—will depend on the type of business and assets you're selling and the type of buyer you seek.

The mountains of paperwork required in selling a business can be daunting. It will seem as if your contracts have contracts as you document due diligence, letters of intent, and purchase/sale agreements, to name only a few. These documents need extensive review and control with extremely competent counsel. Your negotiation demands that you are totally attentive to items that may have lasting consequences for your future. You don't want highly restraining provisions in your noncompete clauses, nor do you want trailing expenses or liabilities because of inexpertly drafted representations and warranties.

Once your business is sold, the liquidity formerly tied up in your company is freed to finance the future you designed earlier in the process. You most likely have had, as a majority of business owners do, a substantial amount of your net worth tied up in your business. As it becomes available, the financial planning we recommended you begin early in the selling process comes to fruition. Here again, specialized senior advisors can help you sort through your options and criteria for decision.

Life after the business is different in ways other than the activities you engage in and the financial structures you adopt. It is common for business owners to have relied on the resources of their business in ways that are no longer available once their business is sold. Family offices or multifamily offices are the vehicles of choice to replace these services and provide oversight on the management of your wealth.

A different situation requiring your special consideration is a merger. It can be simply the linking of two companies or the full integration of two or more business ecosystems. It starts when you identify potential buyers, and your due diligence must include examining their ability to integrate with your organization. Governance and communication throughout the process should be jointly managed using the same management tools as other sophisticated initiatives. But, as our experience has taught us, the acquirer calls the shots.

We started this book saying we had an "ah-ha moment" when we realized that other practitioners and books in the market did not have the holistic, values-based approach that we have found to be so successful with our clients. By stepping back to design your future, you can navigate the process and perils, confidently knowing you'll achieve ultimate success as you have defined it.

Entrepreneurs such as you are not paint-by-numbers people. Entrepreneurs seek to make their own way and their own mark. As management guru Jim Collins puts it:

We all make choices about how we live our lives. You can take a paint-by-numbers approach, or you can start with a blank canvas. When you paint by numbers, the end result is guaranteed. You know what it's going to be, and it might be good, but it will never be a masterpiece. Starting with a blank canvas is the only way to get a masterpiece, but you could also blow up. So, are you going to pick the paint-by-numbers kit or the blank canvas?

You chose a blank canvas, and now your masterpiece is ready to be sold. Congratulations again. Please keep us posted on your journey and join our community by visiting us at www.sellingyourbusinessformore.com. We want to hear from you. It continues to be our pleasure and our lifelong calling to work with and learn from extraordinary people like you.

Afterword

Nothing drives our messages home better than one business owner speaking to another. Mike Nikolich's sale of his public relations firm Tech Image brings to life every lesson we've learned through our decades of serving business owners: timing the market is difficult, be prepared, look at your finances before you start the sale process, bring in top-drawer advisors, design a post-sale role in the business, expect setbacks and learn from them, position your company for sale, remember the importance of communication, and be guided by your values.

Selling Your Business Successfully Requires More Than Luck
By Mike Nikolich, President, Tech Image®

One of my favorite expressions is, "Luck is where preparation meets opportunity." But when I had the opportunity to sell my public relations firm to one of my clients in 2007, I didn't rely on luck to close the deal. To the outside observer, it might appear that I was extremely fortunate. I won't deny that people are lucky, but I'm convinced it was years of preparation that resulted in the smooth sale of Tech Image to SmithBucklin Corporation, the world's largest association management company.

One of the books that had a big impact on me was *The E-Myth* by Michael Gerber. The book teaches you how to position a company for sale by optimizing operations and running your business like a franchise.

As I reflect on the sale of my company, there were six tipping points that helped me create, run, and ultimately sell the company. They included (in order):

- Launching the company
- Managing growth
- Seeking outside advice
- Joining a network of public relations firms

- Surviving an economic downturn
- Packaging the company for sale

Like many small-business owners, when I founded Tech Image in 1993, to quote Gerber, "I was a technician having an entrepreneurial seizure."

Launching the Company

After working fourteen years for other companies, I believed I was smarter than my bosses and wanted the freedom and independence of being the master of my domain. What I didn't account for was how difficult and lonely it was to run a successful business. Although Tech Image was profitable from year one, it took a long time for me to trust the company's sustainability. Starting a company felt like jumping off a cliff without a parachute. Sure, I was a talented public relations professional, but nothing I had done in my career prepared me for the trials and tribulations of running a start-up business. I quickly understood why 50 percent of startups fail after the first year and 50 percent of the survivors fail in year two.

Managing Growth

As a technology-focused public relations firm, we rode the wave of growth that was fueled by companies like IBM, Microsoft, and Apple during the 1990s. The agency grew by 30 percent per year for the first five years and was profitable from day one. On paper, we were successful, but unstable personnel and the constant hunt for new clients stressed me out more than I ever imagined.

It wasn't until I hired Dennis Collins, a former client, as my chief operating officer that things began to settle down. Dennis is a marketing whiz and a rare individual who can balance the creative and financial sides of business. In addition, he was trained to use a personality assessment tool, which we used to help recruit and retain the right employees.

For years, we hired mostly junior level public relations (PR) professionals and had an employee churn rate of almost 50 percent annually. Our offices are located in suburban Chicago, and most of our employees were reverse commuting from the city. Suddenly, the solution was obvious—hire senior-level public relations professionals who live within ten miles of the office. This simple fix, coupled with our use of the assessment tool, helped us all but eliminate turnover. Many of the people we hired after Dennis joined the company are still working at Tech Image today.

In 1999, one of our major competitors was acquired by a multinational firm. Although I did not know the seller personally, I invited her to lunch. She graciously shared many of the details of selling her company, and we quickly became friends. This discussion gave me a much keener insight into the mergers and acquisitions process. I recounted her story to Dennis, and we wondered whether the time was right to sell Tech Image. Despite the fact that Dennis moved his family from Indianapolis to Chicago to work for me, he was not at all intimidated by the thought of selling the company. Since my wife Susan and I were the sole shareholders of Tech Image, I met with my advisory team to explore ideas for rewarding Dennis in the event of a sale. We created an equity rights agreement whereby Dennis's ownership share would vest over a four-year period.

Seeking Outside Advice

The next step was to hire a New York-based consultant to provide a business valuation of Tech Image. His methodology was based on a formula used by large multinational agencies to acquire smaller firms. The purchase price was based on a multiple of earnings before interest, taxes, depreciation, and amortization (EBITDA). The typical transaction consists of a down payment that ranges from 25 percent to 35 percent of the purchase price and an earn-out period of three to five years. To maximize the earn-out, sellers are expected to continue running the company throughout the earn-out period.

Initially, I was underwhelmed by the value the consultant placed on Tech Image, but what owner wouldn't believe his or her company is worth more than it probably is? However, the process paid off when a large multinational public relations firm expressed interest in buying Tech Image in 2000. The acquisition team wanted someone to head its Chicago office and also wanted to expand its technology PR offerings. The discussions led to a preliminary offer that was very close to the consultant's valuation.

Fortunately, as it turned out, a term sheet never materialized. Even though I wasn't knocked out by the offer, the experience was invaluable. It forced me to think about what was important. By our third discussion with the buyers it became very apparent that they were not as interested in my company as they were having me run their Chicago office. They also weren't committed to servicing technology clients, and most of our existing clients were too small to fit their pricing model. In short, the fit was wrong, and selling my firm to this company would have been a disaster.

My suspicions were confirmed when the market crashed in 2001. Our billings dropped nearly 50 percent in 2002 and 2003. Had I sold the company in 2000, I would have received the 30 percent down payment and no additional earn-out payments. It's very likely I would have lost my job or at least be forced to reduce headcount. (By the way, none of the executives from the negotiating team was employed by the buyer in 2002.)

As an independent agency, we survived the downturn by adjusting our business model without reducing headcount. This positioned the agency for explosive growth when the market rebounded during the fall of 2003. After meeting with a second consultant, Dennis and I agreed that Tech Image needed to at least double its billings and EBITDA to receive a fair offer for the business.

Joining a Network of PR Firms

To accelerate sales, we took a hard look at our business. Since we were still a small boutique agency, we became interested in joining a network of independent PR firms. Our research and a recommendation from a writer at *PR Week* led us to apply for membership in the WorldCom Public Relations Group. This move would have a profound impact on our future. Being part of the network gave us access to more than 1,000 public relations professionals in more than thirty-five countries on all continents. We continued to position Tech Image as a boutique agency but also used WorldCom to enhance our sales and marketing efforts.

Another major benefit was being able to network with other agency CEOs, many of whom previously had sold or purchased agencies. We shared best practices and discussed strategies for growing and selling our businesses.

Surviving the Economic Downturn of 2001

I remember having dinner with a business consultant at the WorldCom meeting in Puerto Vallarta, Mexico, in late 2003. Business was improving, and it was obvious that the agency had survived the dot-com bust of 2001, yet I was frustrated. A couple of margaritas later I had one of those "ah-ha" moments. I had spent so much of the previous three years keeping the business afloat that, career-wise, I was adrift. The consultant urged me to spend time thinking about what I wanted from Tech Image and to consciously thank the business for what it was providing me. About two months later, I was attending an investment seminar. As I crossed LaSalle Street in Chicago, I thanked the business for providing me with an income and the flexibility to attend the seminar. I called up the consultant and said I knew what I wanted to do with Tech Image—sell the business. He thought I was crazy.

Positioning the Company for Sale

I shared this revelation with Dennis in January 2004, and we began positioning the company for sale. I rewrote the business plan and, for the first time, it included an exit strategy (selling the company). Against the advice of my advisors, I shared this information with my employees at our annual retreat in 2004. My message was simple: the business was ten years old, and I had managed it through boom and bust periods. Simply growing the business from X to Y was not going to motivate me. I needed to explore an exit strategy, including the possibility of creating an employee stock ownership plan (ESOP) or selling Tech Image to another company. I also made it clear that I planned to be part of the transition team when I sold the business and that I would not target other PR firms, unless the fit was perfect.

Crystallizing this decision reenergized me. Dennis and I spent months working on the business, including redesigning the Web site, updating our logo, and even moving into upscale new offices in downtown Buffalo Grove, a suburb of Chicago. We hired a sales consultant to help us develop comprehensive sales and marketing strategies to attract midsized technology clients and, based on his recommendation, hired Mary Eggert as our director of business development.

Mary spent the next six months presenting our capabilities to prospects, and based on her feedback we installed a new customer relationship management system (CRM) to manage our new business efforts. We also created new case studies and brochures, based on Mary's input.

The business took off in 2005, and we never looked back. Tech Image continued to be one of the few tech-focused public relations firms in the Chicago area, and Dennis and I knew it would only be a matter of time before an opportunity to sell the company presented itself.

That year, I attended a WorldCom Public Relations Group meeting in New York City and met a mergers and acquisitions attorney named Brad Schwartzberg. Brad led a session on selling your agency, and he opened my eyes to the tax advantages of stock-based sales versus asset-based sales.

We hired a new consultant to perform a second business valuation. Now that we knew what the company was worth and the strategies we needed to follow to drive growth, we were ready if the opportunity to sell the company arose.

Fortuitous Meeting

In March 2006, I had my annual lunch with Cindy Kuhn, senior vice president of marketing and communications services at SmithBucklin, one of our largest clients. Cindy had hired Tech Image in 2003 to provide public relations services for several of SmithBucklin's association clients. During lunch, I mentioned my interest in exploring an ESOP option for Tech Image. Cindy chuckled and remarked that SmithBucklin had just completed an ESOP, and she offered to link me up with her CEO, Henry Givray.

Three months later, Henry and I were having lunch and discussing the mechanics of ESOPs, including the costs. As lunch concluded, Henry paused and said, "I may have a better option for you. Why don't we acquire Tech Image? That way, all of your employees can participate in the SmithBucklin ESOP."

I was intrigued but also had many reservations about selling Tech Image to one of my clients.

- Was I really ready to sell the company?
- What happened if the deal fell through?
- How would my other clients react?
- Did my employees want to work for SmithBucklin, the world's largest association management company?
- What would I do with the rest of my life?

Ready to Negotiate

Since I already had been through the process, I knew what to expect when negotiations with SmithBucklin got serious. We had just completed a fresh business
valuation and used a sophisticated accounting software package to manage our
business. As a result, it was easy to respond quickly to SmithBucklin's requests
for financial information, client references, business plans, and so on. Most
requests took less than two hours to process. It wasn't that we were overeager; we
were simply prepared. And, isn't luck where preparation meets opportunity?

After Henry Givray made an initial offer, I hired Brad Schwartzberg to complete the negotiations. Since I planned to work for the company after the sale,
I did not want to get emotionally involved in the negotiations. I also asked for
Henry's assurance that SmithBucklin would continue using Tech Image as a
vendor, even if the deal fell through. Henry's guarantee made me very confident
this deal would reach a successful conclusion.

The initial offer was made in September, and we signed a term sheet in
October. At that point, I sat down with my employees and let them know what
was happening. Henry did the same for SmithBucklin's employees. We worked
closely with SmithBucklin's corporate marketing department to create a communications strategy for both organizations. More than 750 employees at both
companies, plus all of my clients, knew about the sale for nearly three months,
and not a single word was leaked outside until SmithBucklin announced the
news in January 2007.

To ease any concerns by Tech Image employees, Henry met collectively and
individually with everyone during the due diligence process. He was pleasantly surprised to learn that nearly half of us had applied for jobs or worked at
SmithBucklin at some point in our careers!

Successful Sale

All Tech Image employees and clients stayed with the agency after the sale.
During 2006, Tech Image was named "Best Boutique Agency to Work for" by the
Holmes Report, a prestigious national organization. We won this award again in
2007 (after being acquired) and finished second in 2008 and 2009. What's more
significant, all Tech Image employees participated in the SmithBucklin ESOP.
Henry has commented more than once that Tech Image deeply understands and
fully embraces SmithBucklin's vision, mission, chosen values, and business drivers, including the importance and privilege of employee ownership.

Once the deal closed, it took fewer than six months to integrate operations with SmithBucklin, including human resources, IT, and accounting.
SmithBucklin allowed Tech Image to retain its brand and identity (you'd be
hard-pressed to find a mention of the company on the Tech Image Web site).
And we have been encouraged and enabled to continue to apply the business
practices and principles that have made Tech Image successful. However, Tech

Image also has been able to leverage and take full advantage of SmithBucklin's significant resources, knowledge, and infrastructure.

I became a member of SmithBucklin's senior management team. The closer I worked with these colleagues, the more excited I became about the synergies between our two companies. Perhaps more important, I was heartened to discover that we in fact did share the same values. SmithBucklin has been in business nearly sixty years and has a first-rate management team and well-documented best practices. Several Tech Image employees (including me) have tapped into their best practices and training to become much more effective managers.

When Tech Image's business flattened in 2007, Al Koob, SmithBucklin's CFO, took me under his wing and helped me optimize operations to maximize the earn-out. Our business took off again in 2008 and 2009, and today Tech Image is one of SmithBucklin's top-performing operating units.

Synergies of the Sale

I believe Tech Image is a much stronger company as an operating unit of SmithBucklin than we were as an independent business. We are backed by the resources of a $100 million company, which improves our ability to grow our business and deliver better client service. In addition, Tech Image employees now have more career path opportunities, receive competitive salaries and benefits, and are able to become owners by participating in a well-run ESOP.

With the growth of social networking tools like Facebook and Twitter, Tech Image is evolving into a Web 2.0 content company. Although public relations will always be in our DNA, we hope to provide social networking solutions to all of SmithBucklin's client associations in the years ahead. This opportunity would not have been possible prior to us being acquired by them.

Although I often hear horror stories about business acquisitions going bad, as I reflect on selling Tech Image to SmithBucklin in 2006 I couldn't be happier or more excited about the future for Tech Image and its employees as well as for me personally. Beginning in 2010, I will become SmithBucklin's chief marketing officer. Dennis will succeed me as president of Tech Image.

Takeaway Lessons

The lessons I learned from this experience:

- Be prepared. Know what your company is worth. Develop an exit strategy and know what you want to do after you sell your company.
- Study the financial and taxation ramifications of the transaction before you receive an offer. I began working with financial advisors before and after the sale. Their advice helped me minimize my tax burden and maximize my return from this deal.

- Keep your employees informed and champion their best interests. One of the things I am most proud of is the fact that my employees still work for Tech Image and are employee-owners of SmithBucklin.
- Don't view the potential of the sale through rose-colored glasses. You can't control economic downturns, and it's impossible to predict the future. Be pragmatic when you mull over the offer. Insist on having control over your business throughout the earn-out period. You'll never have this opportunity again.
- Visualize the perfect suitor. When I think about the attributes of the type of company I wanted to sell Tech Image to, it's hard to visualize a better fit than SmithBucklin.

Carefully select an expert team of consultants to assist you. My advisors included an accountant, a banker, and an M and A attorney, and we worked together as a team to conclude this transaction successfully.

Index